MIGRATIONS
and other short stories

Joan L. Dow

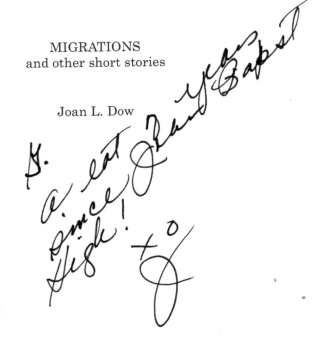

ISBN : 978-148102682

Dedication

This book is dedicated to my grandchildren
Marcie, Jeramy, Logan and Riley

and great grandchildren
Nola Joan & Simon Alphee

in the hope that they, too, will write their stories.

These stories are glimpses of the grace, humor,
loss and love that surround us,
seen through my inner eye over my seventy years.
Some are recalled and some just imagined.
If you find yourself here,
you are the inspiration, not the character.

Special thanks to my writer friends
Pearl Sawyer and Ann Hillis for their support
&
Maureen Rafferty for her editing, cheerleading
and proofreading skills
&
Monica Woods and Dianne Benedict for their inspiration
&
Mary Oliver, my sister, for the watercolor cover
&
Pomie MacVane for the graphic design
&
Dr. A for steadfast encouragement

That Sunday Morning
– 1945 –

Every Sunday morning at precisely quarter past eight, the
front door of our house would open and our family would walk
hurriedly, single file, across the narrow porch that ran along the side
of our three-story, yellow frame house. This particular Sunday was
no exception. We were dressed in our very best, and every head,
including Dad's, was topped with a new spring hat. My sisters and I
wore brimmed creations trimmed with flowers, held fast by a narrow,
elastic cord hidden under our long hair. My baby sister Annie's bonnet
was tied with pink satin matching the rosebuds embroidered on her
white, smocked dress.

We three girls in our floral dresses walked down the front
steps slowly and paused on the sidewalk, waiting. My small mother,
grasping our baby tightly, carefully came down the porch steps on new,
white high-heeled shoes, a shiny white pocketbook dangling from her
arm. Dad came last, bouncing the wicker stroller down the steps in
front of him, its squeaks and squawks sounding like an angry chicken.
He turned the stroller in the direction we would be walking and
arranged the cushions. "Put the baby in," he said. "We'll be late for
church." Dad was a practical man, and he wore a practical, brown suit
along with his white shirt and brown-and-blue-striped tie. He helped
Mum settle the baby.

"Can I push the stroller, Daddy?" asked my next-to-the-youngest
sister Mia, age six. She hopped on one foot, her black braids swinging
toward her delicate face.

Dad rearranged the silent baby. "No. I told Tess she could."

1

Tess, age ten, had already placed her hands just so, waiting to walk, waiting to push the baby's carriage. She was the image of Mum – wide-set blue eyes, porcelain skin and dark hair.

"Can I push it on the way home?" asked Mia, now twirling her wide braids, one in each hand.

"We'll see," said my father. He stood back admiring the beautiful baby.

Mia turned to me. "I'm going to push the stroller on the way home, Jo," she said. Not long ago she was the baby, and she still retained a scrap of this prestige.

"He said we'll see," I said, knowing we'll see meant probably not. I knew a lot from Dad's tone of voice. I was seven and struggled to be exemplary in the presence of our parents. I pursed my lips, concealing my rather large front teeth.

"It's my turn next," continued Mia. "I never get to push the baby. You take the baby out every afternoon."

"Stop whining," said Dad. He straightened his broad-brimmed hat. "Jo and Mia, you two hold hands and walk in front. Tess, you and the baby go next. Mother and I will walk behind." He removed his glasses and held them up, squinting, searching for dust specks. "There is to be no loud talking or skipping on the way to church." He blew on one of his lenses, then put the glasses back on, guiding the gold wires behind his ears. He glanced at his watch. We were right on time.

Our little procession headed down Main Street, past the red-brick fire station with the wide-open door, past the Beer Garden with the chairs upside down on the tabletops next to the big window. At Robinson's Grocery, Mr. Robinson, his large wraparound apron pure white at this hour, was carrying in the bundle of Sunday papers. "Mornin'," Mr. Robinson huffed. His thinning, sandy hair was already damp with perspiration. "There's good news today," he said, turning the bundle toward our family so that the headline could be read:

2

"Italian Partisans Kill Mussolini."

Mum gasped. Her hand flew to the broach of the Blessed Mother Mary pinned at the neck of her organza dress. It froze there before she continued to where our family waited.

Dad shifted from foot to foot, pacing time. "We'll be picking up our paper on the way back, Mr. Robinson," he said.

There would be no good news about the war until Mum's two brothers came home. I was sure the II in World War II referred to my two uncles. She glanced down at the sidewalk and saw where a dropped tomato had sprung up as a plant in a crack in the sidewalk, next to the vegetable stand. "Look, girls," she said. "See how God creates little miracles!" We all stared at the plant for a moment, then walked on.

"Let's keep up with the girls," Dad said, cupping Mum's elbow in the palm of his hand to gently urge her forward.

The heavy scent of fuel hung on the air as we walked on past the coal barn, its top dark and weathered. Two empty windows flanked the rickety ramp where trucks backed in to dump coal down the open chutes to the gasworks below.

Yesterday, my friend Kenny and I had played "airplane" there. We had tiptoed in across the loose beams. My shoe had hit a piece of coal, and it skittered off the beam and tumbled down a stack of coal, sounding like a rifle shot down a canyon. We had waited motionlessly, but the workers did not look up. Dusty pigeons overhead saw us and murmured from the rafters. Kenny and I had moved cautiously over the loose floorboards, on to the end of the barn. Each step rattled or creaked.

"C'mon, Kenny. I'll tie on your blindfold. Then we'll run until we fly."

Kenny began to stutter so I asked, "Do you just want to watch me fly today?" Kenny nodded, and I tied on one of my father's handkerchiefs and ran the length of the barn, with arms outstretched like wings, until I stumbled and fell through one of the chutes in the floor. Down I tumbled along the tower of coal, blindfolded and bruised, sliding on my knees to the dirt floor two stories below. A whistle blew and through the steam two sooty workers came running: one was waving a rake; the other, a shovel. Their clothes and faces were smeared with soot. The tall, thin one, his mouth a red hole in his face, yelled, "Get out of here before we boil ya' in tar!"

The fat one with the shovel grabbed my arm, but I pulled away and ran behind the bins. Then I slipped under the fence into Mr. O'Connell's yard. Sometimes, Mr. O'Connell would come out and yell, "I'm gonna call the cops if y'ever run through here again." That day, no one came out. I ran up on Main Street, but Kenny was gone.

Now, walking to church, my dress just covered the scrapes on my knees from the precarious flight of the day before. At the corner, the O'Connells came out of their small, white house. Mrs. O'Connell was an enormous, red-headed lump of a woman held up on dainty feet, always breathless and incapable of hurrying. Mr. O'Connell was a fireman who accidentally set his house afire twice while stoking his woodstove. When he wasn't at the fire station, he was seated in the window at the Beer Garden, drinking and listening to saloon songs on the player piano.

Watching him, I was reminded of how often I stopped at the Beer Garden and sat on the bench out front, pushing the stroller back and forth. I would sing to my baby sister at the top of my voice while the piano plinked until someone staggered out of the Beer Garden and gave me money. It was usually a dime, which I would spend next door at Robinson's store on an ice cream for myself and Annie. Now Mr. O'Connell bent down to look at our baby, thrusting his puffy, red face into the front of the stroller. "How old is the baby now?" he asked.

"She just turned two," I said.

"She's a beauty!" said Mr. O'Connell, standing upright again. "Does she talk yet?" he asked.

4

"She doesn't need to," said Tess. "We know what she wants."

"You managed to get three Irish ones," Mr. O'Connell said. The big, blue-eyed baby blinked, then tossed her head back, her bonnet slipping off the shiny black curls. She arched her back and turned to look at me.

Tess stepped from behind the stroller, sliding the bonnet back in place. "We are French and Irish, Mr. O'Connell," she said. Mum smiled her tiny bit of a smile.

Mr. O'Connell, his pale eyes rimmed red, said, "Not that one," pointing to me. "Where did you get the blondie?"

Mia said brightly, "Daddy said she came to us tied on the back of a yellow dog."

"That's a lie!" I said.

Mia smiled up at the O'Connells. "It's true, isn't it, Daddy?"

"It's true all right," he said, straightening his hat. "Now, let's keep moving. We don't want to be late." The O'Connells began to walk with us. Dad checked his pocket watch.

Four years ago our mother had made a vow to Saint Ann that, if she could have just one more baby (perhaps a boy?), she would make three kind comments every Sunday in gratitude. Mrs. O'Connell offered her the first opportunity of the day. Mrs. O'Connell was wearing a red, pleated dress and a small, orange straw hat, and she was carrying a square yellow pocketbook. "Mrs. O'Connell, you look like a woman in a painting," Mum said.

Mrs. O'Connell, wheezing from trying to keep up, gasped, "Why thank you, Mrs. LaFlamme." Her smile revealed small, square teeth, and she stopped to secure her hat on top of her sausage-like curls. Our family dutifully marched on.

From Davis Street and all the rest of the way to the corner where we would turn, the elm trees on both sides of Main Street had leafed out and joined hands above the sidewalk. The sun flickered down on our family, bringing warmth to the late May morning. Mum reached down and unbuttoned the baby's white sweater.

Gertie Reagan, in her usual state of high anxiety, flew by us, swinging her pocketbook over her head. Gertie lived one street away from us in a tiny little frame house that had never seen a paintbrush, up high on a hill that had never seen a lawn mower. I would walk all the way there to discard a candy wrapper on her lawn, hoping for a glimpse of Gertie. Sometimes Gertie chased me all the way to the gasworks where I would slip from sight. That day Gertie stopped just beyond us in the middle of the sidewalk, turned in a crouch and yelled at me, "You dirty little bastard! You better keep off my lawn or I'll rip out your gizzard!"

Our family parade stopped in its tracks. "There will be none of that today, Gertie," said Dad, his vision of a perfect day evaporating. "Now move on or I'll have to speak to Father Nelligan." Gertie flounced up her dress, revealing long, peach, ribbed undies and galloped down the street, swinging her pocketbook as if she were riding a runaway horse.

"Saints preserve us!" whispered Mum.

Soon more parishioners walking to church joined the parade. Women in floral hats with little veils walked alongside men in straw hats, who touched the brims with their right hands whenever they said hello. Conversations traveled back and forth, connected by *good mornings.*

I saw Kenny's house and hoped his dog was locked inside. Often when we walked home from school, Kenny's mean little dog would run toward us, and no amount of coaxing could prevent the inevitable. The dog always bit somebody, and usually it was Kenny. Last week, as I was walking home with Kenny, I had seen his dog lying in the gutter in front of Mr. Robinson's store. He was almost entirely covered with leaves. I had said, "Oh, my goodness, Kenny. Your dog got run over." Kenny had rushed to the dog and knelt beside him. The dog had leapt up and bit his arm.

Now Kenny came out of his yard and waited for me. His dark hair was damp and brushed to one side. He had on a new, white shirt and a blue-and-red-striped necktie, a real tie that he had tied himself.

"Hi, Kenny," I said. "Do you want to walk with us?"

A screen door slammed and Kenny's little brown dog shot down the yard with his head tilted and his teeth set for Kenny's shin. I called loudly, "Mrs. Williams, would you please call Kenny's dog?" The dog sunk his teeth into Kenny's brown corduroy pants and, while Kenny kicked his leg as hard as he could, the dog held fast. Then a car drove by and tooted. The dog, built like a meat loaf, released his grip on the corduroys as he dashed into the road after the car. The driver, trying to avoid the dog, nicked him with the bumper. The dog collapsed just ahead of our family at the side of the road. "Oh, my goodness," I yelled. "Now your dog has really been run over."

Our entire family stopped. Mum gasped, "Is he...dead?"

Kenny started to cry, we girls began to cry, the baby sat up and stared. Mr. Williams came out of the house as Kenny ran back into his yard.

"Get in the car, Kenny," he said. Kenny got in, glad to get away from the vicious meat loaf. The car backed out and soon had turned the corner.

As we neared the dog laying in the gutter, we heard a low growl. Dad, with a tinge of disappointment in his voice, said, "Just what we need – a dog miracle!" The dog jumped up and raced home like he had been hurled from a catapult. Everyone stopped crying. Then I began to skip. Mia joined in, our black elastic cords keeping our hats a beat behind our steps. We chanted, If you step on a crack...you'll break your mother's back!

"Walk, you two. No skipping," said my father. "And there is to be no talking in church."

"OK, Daddy," said Mia.

"Just sit there and be quiet."

"OK, Daddy," repeated Mia.

"And don't plague the baby," he said in the same low voice. "Did you hear me, Jo?"

"Yes, Daddy." I heard every word he ever said to me.

We turned the corner and walked up Cedar Street. Old Father Nelligan was standing near the open double-doors, greeting the faithful as they arrived at Saint Mary's for the nine o'clock Mass. His eyes, beneath papery eyelids, looked perpetually surprised as if becoming an old priest with pastel-pink hair in a flowing, black cassock had happened to him accidentally. His arms flew up when he saw the family with the four daughters. "Ah, the LaFlammes!" he said.

Mum smiled her half smile. "Good morning, Father Nelligan. The new loudspeaker system is a big improvement," she said, fulfilling her second compliment of the day. "We always sit down front, as you know, but last Sunday everyone could hear your sermon, even out in the churchyard. I'm looking forward to every word today."

"As am I, Mrs. LaFlamme," said Father Nelligan, leaning over the stroller. He reached out a parchment hand to touch Annie's head just as our father picked her up. Tess, still very much in charge of the stroller, jerked it forward as she backed up the wide, granite stairs and pulled it into the vestibule. Quite a crowd was gathered there, some picking up the church bulletin, some waiting for friends. She parked the stroller near the gray marble holy water font, and Dad secured the hand brake against the back wheel.

Mum teetered up the steps in her new shoes to join us and began to straighten and smooth each girl's outfit. "Jo, how did you manage to wrinkle your dress?" she asked while rubbing her white-gloved hand back and forth across my skirt of rumpled flowers, willing it to become smooth. I didn't even blink, just endured. The two tall,

8

thin McClay sisters in parrot feather hats stopped to admire us. Mum responded to their compliments with uncertainty, wanting to believe they were true. She twisted the silver buckle to open her ample pocketbook and began handing out small prayer books.

"Can I have the blue one?" asked Mia, pulling on Mum's sleeve. "I never get the blue one." Mum grabbed the blue prayer book with the Blessed Mother on it from my hand and gave it to Mia. Then she turned back and said to me, "Here, dear. You can use mine today."

"Now," said Dad, passing our big baby to our small mother, "are you girls going to behave today?"

"Yes, Daddy," said Mia, reaching for his hand.

"Yes, Daddy," said Tess, smiling her very best smile.

"Jo?" said father, removing his hat. I nodded my head. "Then let's go in. I don't want to hear a peep out of any of you." An exemplary family was for him the mark of a successful man.

We walked single file down the red-tiled center aisle, led by Dad. Mum was last, carrying our beautiful baby. The air was still laden with incense from the earlier Mass. Dad genuflected, then turned to usher his brood into the second pew from the front. We three girls, kneeling silently, resting our heads on the seat in front, were like a row of topiary trees.

Mother put her pocketbook on the kneeler next to father's hat and placed the baby on the seat between them. The baby turned and pulled herself up, her firm, freshly whitened shoes knocking against the back of the wooden seat. Kenny, his hair now dry and porcupine-like, was seated two rows back next to the McClay sisters, their green feathered hats gleaming. The baby stood there, all pink and white, grasping the furled seat back with her chubby hands, looking back as parishioners filed quietly into their seats. The baby's mouth formed an O. Her bonnet slipped off as she began to sway. And it was then that she began to sing...*I wonder who's buying the wine, for lips that I used to call mine*...while the sun filtered through the stained glass windows like grace from heaven.

A quiet came over the parishioners, who were kneeling now in their pews. Mrs. O'Connell stopped wheezing. Gertie turned and stood as still as the statue of Mother Mary.

I wonder if he ever tells her of me, I wonder who's kissing her now.

Her clear, high voice floated up with the dust motes into the choir loft to the very pinnacle of the ceiling painted with cherubs.

The Day Tubby Condon Ate God
– 1946 –

Every Friday afternoon St. Mary's School marched to the church, grade by grade, to go to Confession. My class, grade 3, went at one o'clock. We marched there silently and alphabetically, the way we sat in class. So Billy LeBree was in front of me. I was followed by Llewellin Moreau, to whom I never dared whisper. No one whispered as we marched. I guess, like me, they were searching through events of the preceding week for mortal sins. Confession was serious business, and the Sisters of Mercy suggested that we only confess our mortals. Perhaps this was because, if we confessed all our venial sins, we'd be there all afternoon.

As soon as we left the school yard and headed by the convent, I'd start with the First Commandment to see if I had a mortal sin against it. I am the Lord, thy God, thou shall not have strange gods before me. Whew! I was sure there had been no strange gods that week. Thou shalt not take the name of the Lord thy God in vain. One mortal. I'd skip over the Third, but always confess the Fourth: Honor Thy Father and Mother. One more mortal. I'd never killed, nor committed adultery, nor stolen a thing. Eight, Nine and Ten had to do with neighbors, and while I wasn't sure what a false witness was, I knew I'd never coveted my neighbor's wife nor goods. As we marched by the black-iron spiked fence, I was wondering if Father Nelligan recognized my voice and my same mortal sins as he heard my Confession each Friday afternoon.

Sister Mary Thecla moved with and against the line from A to S. Joanne Quimbey used to be last until Tim Sawyer stayed back a grade. Sister was always fingering her rosary beads with her right hand and straightening the line with the other.

On this particular warm June afternoon, as we filed into the pews, Tubby Condon left the line. He walked right past the kneeling As and Bs. Behind him, Danny Dwyer just stopped where he was, and the line did not move. Tubby kept walking right up to the altar rail. He unfastened the little brass clasp on the railing and walked without genuflecting right up the altar steps. He opened the bronze tabernacle door and moved the little white curtain to one side. He reached inside and he did it. He ate God. The Big Consecrated Host. He turned around, and we saw him chewing God.

Suddenly Sister Mary Thecla came from the rear of the line, like an enormous bird, flying past Gs, Fs, Es, and Ds. She swooped into the sanctuary, swinging her rosary, and hit Tubby with wooden Hail Mary's. She shook him, but his head did not roll off. He swallowed God.

Sister made Tubby kneel alone on the red tile floor while we went to Confession. Then she opened the door to the confessional and went in with Tubby to be sure Father Nelligan knew what Tubby had done. God already knew.

It was while they were in the confessional that we made the plan. We decided to take turns watching Tubby all that day so one of us would see Tubby get the bolt. Our Bible History books were filled with pictures of God throwing lightning bolts at sinners, even destroying whole cities, for lesser sins than Tubby's.

We marched back to our classroom on the second floor. When it was my turn to watch Tubby, I pretended to read but I didn't even blink. Tubby raised his hand to go to the toilet. Before he left the room, Billy Church stood up and asked to be excused. That was the way we asked to go to the toilet, that's what "to be excused" meant. If Tubby got the bolt in the toilet, Billy would be able to tell us.

When the bell rang at three o'clock, we said our dismissal prayers. Tubby was still alive.

Four of us walked Tubby home, and no one talked until Tubby walked across his porch and inside. Then Jeanne O'Toole said someone should stay at Tubby's for supper and sleep over. No one dared. While we were all standing there, Warren Jr., who wasn't Catholic, came from his yard between my house and Tubby's to see what we were doing. We told him what had happened and what would probably happen during the night. Warren Jr. said he dared to stay over and had stayed up all night once before. We all went home to wait. I wondered if God's bolts would set Tubby's house on fire. I did not sleep well.

The next morning, Tubby was already in the school yard. He was laughing again, and I wondered if God planned to do it when we were not watching. I wondered if maybe God had stopped using bolts.

Trick or Treat
– 1948 –

I opened the back door. There stood Skippy. "Trick or treat," she said, shoving a brown shopping bag toward me.

"You look great. Who are you?" I asked.

"Can't you guess?" Skippy had on a red long-sleeve jersey, a bandanna tied on the side around her neck, and black silk pajama pants. She had slicked back her hair, and I could tell by the smell she had used baby oil. "Tyrone Power, for Gawd's sake."

"I wanted to be Shirley Temple, but my mother didn't get a chance to do my hair in ringlets. Now I don't know what to be. I got this sheet. I could be a ghost," I said and pulled it over my head.

"Forget it," said Skippy. "Everyone who doesn't know what to be will be a ghost. Let's tear it into strips and you can be a mummy!"

She set right to work, making tiny bite marks along the side of the sheet. Then from these little holes she ripped the sheet into long, white mummy cloths. I began wrapping my legs, my torso. I got one arm done before Skippy took over. She ran around me, fastening strips, and said, "I have to cover your eyes to do your head. Then I'll cut out big holes with the scissors."

"Cut the holes first," I said, "I don't want scissors near my eyes."

"Don't be nervous." She ran around me a few more times until I was totally wrapped, eyes and all. "Where does your mother keep the measuring cups?" she asked.

15

I didn't dare move around the kitchen. "In the top drawer in the pantry. Why?" I heard the heavy drawer squeak open and close. Then I felt Skippy place a metal cup over my right eye outlining it with a pencil or a pen. She did the same over my left eye.

"Where are the scissors?" asked Skippy.

Separating the strips, I looked straight into Skippy's gray eyes and said, "Hey, I can see fine. Let's go."

Skippy opened the refrigerator, took out the red Kool-Aid and poured some on the front of me. "Stop! I want to look like a dead mummy, not one that's bleeding to death."

"Now we're ready," said Skippy, and we walked out the back door, leaping across the railing that separated our porch from my grandfather's.

"First we go to Grampy's," I said.

We banged on his door. I heard my grandfather's cane tap the floor, then the drag of his foot as he crossed his kitchen. He opened the door and leaned forward to see us. "Eh, what's your trick?" he asked. His little dog, Chien Noir, growled. Every dog Grampy ever had was a black bull dog named Chien Noir.

"Grampy, it's Skippy and me." Chien Noir jumped up and began licking at the red Kool-Aid.

"Eh, mon dieu, I t'ought the gypsies left you 'ere." Grampy's black beret had lint on it, and I wondered if he was wearing the one he usually wore to bed. He said, "Pink peppermints for you and you," dropping four Canadian wintergreen mints into each bag. Now we could go around the neighborhood! We thundered down his porch stairs and stopped at the sidewalk, then turned down Patten Street.

"Your grandfather looks great tonight, but then he's always dressed for Halloween," said Skippy, poking a peppermint between her jaw and her cheek.

"Where will we start...Fish's house? They always make popcorn balls!"

"OK. But, Gawd! Don't talk. Let 'em guess who we are."

"Not many people are going to say 'Tyrone Power,' Skippy."

We went to Fish's, Jordan's, McLeod's, McNally's, McClay's, Conner's — we went as far as we were allowed to go and began to work our way back on the opposite side of the street. It was just getting dark. The houses were all very similar: white frame with side porches to the front door. We came to Nunny O'Sullivan's and I said, "Shall we go here?"

"Why not?" asked Skippy.

"Sometimes Nunny is glad to see me; sometimes not."

"It's Halloween," said Skippy. "Besides she won't know who you are." Skippy slung her bag of treats over her shoulder and leaned her elbow on the buzzer.

The door flew open and Nunny screamed, "You little bastards, git off my steps or I'll call the cops!" Her white unbraided hair was wavy and wild with the hall light behind her. Then she lifted up a broom and shook it at us. We ran as fast as we could. Some of my mummy bandages unwound and trailed behind us up the street.

"Gawd, she is a real witch!" said Skippy.

"Let's go to Frankie's house. Then we'll go home," I said.

"Remember, you're spending the night at my house."

We walked into Frankie's yard. The back door light was lit, and the storm door, which was on year-round, was open against the side of the house. We knocked a couple of times. The door opened and there was Frankie's mother. She was dazzling. She had red curly hair standing out all around her head. She was wearing a long pink satin robe. Ostrich feathers trimmed the neck and cuffs. "Hi, kids," she said in her low voice, and the feathers near her face danced. "C'mon in."

There, seated at the square kitchen table was a man in his overcoat, his hairy legs tucked under the chair. The only light was from a small, bare bulb above the sink. "This here is one of Frankie's uncles, Uncle Billy. Say hello to the girls, Billy," said Frankie's mother, taking a puff from a cigarette in a long, black, bejeweled holder. She exhaled silver smoke and set the feathers to dancing again.

"Hello, girls," said the uncle, pouring beer from a brown quart bottle into a jelly glass.

"It's me, Mrs. Dunn — and Skippy." Skippy shot me a mean look, as mean as a tiny Tyrone Power could.

"How about a hot dog, honey?" said Frankie's mother, leaning against the table.

"Well, no thanks. We gotta go, Mrs. Dunn," I said.

"Give 'em one for later," said the uncle.

"Here, honey." Mrs. Dunn tossed a cold hot dog in each bag. She walked to the door with us, clicking along in her pink high-heeled slippers trimmed to match her robe.

When we had halfway crossed through the yard, I said, "Isn't Mrs. Dunn just like a movie star?"

"She's got more feathers on her than three ostriches!" said Skippy, reaching into her bag for the hot dog. "Let's go tell your mother we're going to my house now. Do you want to get your pajamas?"

"No. I like the mummy suit. I just need to pick up my clothes for church in the morning."

Sleeping at Skippy's was always an adventure. Her bedroom was on the third floor and had five beds in it, all with different headboards and always made up with Indian blankets instead of bedspreads. She had an older sister and brother who no longer lived at home. Now, Skippy had all the beds, but we always slept together because her bed had an electric blanket on top. The full moon brightened the floor like a floodlight. Suddenly Skippy was asleep. The fudge, popcorn, hot dog and candy lay inside my stomach like a sack of rocks. I had unwrapped my head and loosened the mummy bandages, but I still felt tight in my skin. Then I saw it - a little spark on top on the blanket, next to my feet. It started running in semi-circles back and forth across the blanket like a fuse to dynamite. It ran across our knees. I tried to move but could not. It ran across our stomachs, and I could hear a little hissing sound. As it got closer to the top of the blanket I screamed, "FIRE!" Skippy sat straight up, tossing the covers back, and I jumped up and unplugged the cord.

"Gawd, did you say fire?" asked Skippy, still sitting bolt upright in bed.

"I'm not kidding. The blanket was on fire. Look," I said, pulling back the covers. A curvy, charred path was burned into the pale-yellow blanket. The smell of smoke came up with little, black, fuzzy things floating in it. "We almost burned to death!" I cried.

"We did not. We almost got electrocuted! That's painless," said Skippy. She reached down for her trick-or-treat bag. "Want any candy?"

"I want my mother," I said, starting to cry.

"No, you don't. You just want to go to sleep. Let's take the twin beds over by the window. OK?"

We walked across the cool linoleum floor, got into the beds and pulled up the Indian blankets. I waited quietly for sleep. A cloud slipped in front of the moon, darkening the room. I heard a trashcan tip over and a dog bark. I could still smell the smoke, but mostly I could smell the baby oil in Skippy's hair. The next thing I heard was Skippy's mother calling us to get ready for church.

Pigeons
- 1951 -

My grandfather, Peter LaFlamme, and his neighbor, Albert Burpee, were sitting in green-striped canvas chairs on the high side lawn in the shade of huge elm trees. They had one joint mission in life: to rid the eaves of the house of pigeons. The summer I was thirteen years old was the height of their campaign. As I walked to where they were sitting, my grandfather turned to me and said in his heavy French Canadian accent, "Boys, oh boys, you got 'ere in time to see a terrible t'ing — a pee-john, she is about to die before your eyes."

Mr. Burpee's eyes were riveted to the corner eave on the third floor. He was a tall, gaunt man who leaned to one side as if the wind was pushing against him. All summer Mr. Burpee wore ribbed undershirts — the kind with a scooped out neck and big armholes — and a pair of tan, unironed slacks. This was in sharp contrast to my diminutive grandfather who wore a brocade vest over a white, starched shirt and dark trousers. His one concession to summer was that his shirt was collarless.

My grandfather pointed with his cane and yelled out, "Mon dieu, Burpee, 'ere she comes. 'Er 'ead will get stuck and she'll call out with 'er dying breath, 'Stay away from Pete LaFlamme's 'ouse, or die.' Watch, Burpee."

A dark-gray pigeon with an iridescent neck made a skillful maneuver in midair, landing feet first inside the chicken wire my grandfather had nailed to the front of the eaves to prevent just such a thing. Both men stood up, folded the canvas chairs, and walked silently down the stairs in the steep lawn and into the cellar to devise a new plan.

21

Later, when my friend Skippy came over to teach me how to smoke cigarettes down in our cellar, I could hear my grandfather and Mr. Burpee in his adjoining cellar. My grandfather was singing, "'Oly God, we praise Thy name..." and hammering. These were both bad signs. The last time he sang "Holy God" was when his barrel of homemade wine blew apart. Mr. Burpee was saying things like, "E-e-e-easy" and "I need a rest and a d-d-d-drink."

The following Tuesday, when Skippy and I were walking home from a movie, we saw my grandfather, who was less than five feet tall, creeping up the extension ladder. He would take a step up with his good leg, then drag the other to the same rung. His cane was swinging from the crook in his left arm. In his right hand he was carrying a board with nails driven into it. Mr. Burpee's arms were reaching as high as they could, holding the ladder against the house. It looked as if Mr. Burpee's body was stuttering. He was shaking the ladder.

My grandfather climbed up until he was about level with the eaves and placed the board in it, nail side up. Then he began his descent while Skippy and I watched. Once on the ground, he released the rope and the extension ladder collapsed with a screaming of metal to a regular-size ladder. He and Mr. Burpee carried it down the steps and into the cellar.

"Do you want another smoking lesson?" asked Skippy. She put her shoulder bag down on its side in the steep grass. She took out a see-through plastic case with a pack of Camels and a book of matches.

I looked around, sure that a neighbor was watching, but before I could answer her my grandfather and Mr. Burpee were coming back across the lawn, carrying the canvas chairs. They snapped them open, sat down, and my grandfather called down to us, "Boys, oh boys, a pee-john, she is about to die before your eyes. She will land in the eaves, sink down on the bed of nail and with 'er last breath she will call out, 'Don't come to Pete LaFlamme's 'ouse or you'll bleed to death on a bed of nail!' You watch, girls. It will be a terrible t'ing."

Mr. Burpee leaned back, his sparse hair plastered with sweat against his head, and he squinted at the torturous device up in the eaves. Skippy gripped her pocketbook. "Gawd," she said, "this might be better than the movie!" We crawled up the grassy hill and sat near their chairs. I got out my handkerchief so I could cover my eyes if the sight was too much to stomach. Skippy and Mr. Burpee stared without blinking. A breeze visited the row of elms across the top of the bank, and the leaves rustled like taffeta. A white pigeon with tan splotches approached the eaves, back peddling with her wings, and daintily placed her feet on the nails. Then she just squatted down and cooed the sound that drove my grandfather to these extremes. He and Mr. Burpee got up slowly, folded the chairs, and returned to the cellar.

Skippy said, "He must have put the nails too close together." Skippy was the most informed, modern person I knew, and she already wore a bra and high-heeled shoes to school. Her long, light-brown hair draped down over one eye, mysteriously, like Veronica Lake. When boys were around, she tossed her head about like a pony. "Let's go down in your cellar so we can hear what they are up to."

"Sure," I said, a little disappointed in the pigeon plot. "You can give me another smoking lesson. I want to blow smoke out my nose like they do in the movies."

"You're not ready for that," said Skippy. "You can't even inhale without coughing your brains out."

The next day Skippy and I were on my family's back porch painting our toenails. "Your house and your grandfather's are like mirror images," said Skippy. "If you could pull them apart, you'd have two identical three-story houses."

"Pass me the cotton balls," I said and quickly began wadding them between my toes. Then I heard the cellar door open below. I bent forward, and through a crack in the porch floor I could see my grandfather come out, hauling an end of the extension ladder.

It clanked and clunked until Mr. Burpee appeared holding up the other end.

Skippy said, "Gawd! Here they go again!"

"Let's just paint our toenails. We'll go over after they put the ladder away. I'd rather not watch Grampy climb way up to the eaves again. Where did you get this great orange polish?" I asked.

"Why does your grandfather hate birds?" Skippy asked from behind a wall of hair that hung down as she bent forward to paint.

"He doesn't. He has a canary in his front parlor. He just hates pigeons."

"Why?"

"Grampy says they are nasty, filthy birds with mournful voices. He says they can wake the dead."

"Are you going to paint your fingernails?"

"No! My mother would have a fit, and I wouldn't get out for days."

We took turns painting. It wasn't long until I heard the ladder rattling like pots and pans.

"C'mon," said Skippy. "Let's check out the latest pigeon-killing device."

We hopped over the dividing railing to Grampy's porch and went down his side steps to the lawn. Mr. Burpee was already seated, his eyes fixed upward.

Grampy was just putting his gold watch into his vest pocket when he saw us. "Girls, girls, you are just in time to see a terrible t'ing. Boys, oh boys, a pee-john she's 'bout to die before your eyes."

"How?" asked Skippy.

Grampy turned with a little hop and sunk down into the canvas chair. He jabbed at a bug with the tip of his cane. "Today," he said, "when the pee-john she come, she land on fly paper — that holds 'er down. Then she sink in the bed of nail. With 'er last breath, she calls out, "Don't go to Pete LaFlamme's 'ouse or you die. That's that, eh, Burpee?"

Mr. Burpee patted his thinning hair and stuttered, "Today's the day."

The sun was directly overhead when we saw the silhouette of the pigeon as though it was made of black tin. We could see the broad white band under its rounded tail feathers, which it tipped as if in a pirouette. It landed in the eaves, behind the wire, on top of the fly paper, on the bed of nails. We were hardly breathing, looking up in the heat of the day, as the pigeon flew off with the fly paper hanging off one of its feet.

Grampy stood up and slowly folded his chair. "Mon seigneur," he said.

Mr. Burpee picked up the other chair and followed Grampy down the steps and into the cellar.

I looked down and saw that all the cotton balls between my toes were stuck in the orange polish.

The following day, when Skippy and I were walking back from the store with ice cream, we saw fire trucks with their lights flashing. "Gawd," said Skippy.

"Let's run," I said. "They're in front of my house!"

My ice cream quickly fell out of the cone, but Skippy ran with her tongue pressing down on hers. The hook and ladder truck had its rig on the side street below the lawn. A fireman in a cherry picker was near the top of one of the elms. Lots of other firemen, with nothing to do, were sitting on the lawn. Mr. Burpee was sitting on the front porch steps with his back to the crowd that had gathered on Main Street in front of our house.

Skippy took a big lick of her ice cream and said to the fireman standing near the truck, "What happened?"

"We came thinking there was a fire. Then we thought we were to rescue a cat. We found old Mr. LaFlamme hanging on to a ladder that had tipped backwards into one of these trees."

"Gawd," said Skippy between licks.

"Is he OK?" I asked.

"He's fine. They're bringing him down now. Just a few scratches. He was worried because he dropped his cane. Don't that beat all? A crippled, old guy on a ladder can't find his cane! Somebody ought to hide his ladder."

"The problem is the pigeons," I said. "My grandfather goes up into the eaves after pigeons." And I burst into sobs, told him some of the misadventures, and rubbed my nose on the back of my hand. Skippy looked at me with disgust.

The fireman patted my head and said, "Well, we can fix that while we're here. Now, don't you cry, little girl." He talked to one of the firemen sitting on the lawn and, by the time they left, there were boards covering both eaves on my grandfather's side of the house.

The following day was Sunday, and I was up in my bedroom on the third floor at the front of our house. I heard horns blaring and put down the True Confessions magazine Skippy had lent me to look down at Main Street. My grandfather was in the middle of four lanes of cars, cane dangling from his arm, balancing what looked to be a sixty-foot pole. He took a step backwards and walked in front of a car. A horn blared. Then he tottered forward. Brakes squealed. The pole, with one end stuck in his watch pocket, began to weave from side to side. He took a few more steps, like a flag bearer staggering under the weight, and the pole whipped forward and crashed through my bedroom window. He dropped the pole. A car ran over it and the driver yelled out his window. My grandfather walked with great dignity to the sidewalk as if nothing had happened.

Mr. Burpee rounded the corner. "What's going on?" he stammered.

"My granddaughter 'as been throwing rocks. There's a 'ole in 'er bedroom window the size of a bamboo pole."

The pigeons, now packed into the eaves on either side of my window were coo-cooing loudly. I decided to finish reading about the big-busted woman in the honky-tonk road stop before I went down to tell my parents about the window.

The Supper Party
- 1961 -

In the spring of 1961, Maxine and I left my hometown of Bangor
for her hometown of Presque Isle. We were going up for the weekend
to stay with Maxine's brother Pat and his wife, Rita, and we were going
in style. We were both married to officers in the US Air Force: that
already made us special. We were driving up in Maxine's husband's
brand-new station wagon. and we had dyed our hair pink. Actually,
we hadn't planned on pink hair. We had bought something called
"champagne beige" and it came out pink. Then we dyed Maxine's
French poodle, LaPetite, with pink doggy dye. We teased our hair and
stacked it up in a bee-hive, put on silk Capri pants, and headed for the
County. (That's what everyone in Maine calls Aroostook County, even
though there are fifteen other counties in Maine.)

I wouldn't want you to think the County is backward, but I don't
think anyone up there had ever seen pink hair. It took four hours to
drive there, about the same amount of time it would have taken us to
drive to Boston — that's how far it is to Presque Isle from Bangor. We
had a cooler with bottles of Coca-Cola and some little sandwiches that
I had cut the crusts off, then wrapped individually in waxed paper.

We were both twenty-three years old and had left our young
babies with my mother for the overnight. Our husbands had flown
off somewhere on a mission, and we were off on an adventure of our
own. Maxine was a great driver. She could talk, chew a sandwich,
balance a Coke between her knees, and drive. Sometimes we just
turned up the radio, rolled down the window, and smoked filtered
cigarettes. We felt like a couple of fashion models, and we thought we
looked like them, too.

We had been driving for several hours when the tire on the front passenger side blew out. We lurched to the side of the road and got out and stared at it.

"Do you know how to change a tire?" I asked.

"No," Max answered, "and I don't imagine you do either. We'll just roll through the woods to the next town. There's a Shell station there, and they know my father. We can get it fixed and pick up a spare."

We turned up the radio and rolled all the way to Macwahoc. We crossed the railroad tracks, leaving another ribbon of the tire behind, heard the rim dent in, and pulled into the service station. The attendant wiped his hands on the back of his dark-blue pants, crouched down, and put his face close to Maxine's. He looked at us, at the dog chewing on a peach, blinked a couple of times and said, "You folks in town for the funeral?"

In less than an hour, we were again headed north. When we drove into Maxine's family's driveway, her sister-in-law ran out and said, "Don't park in the yard. Park on the street. Pat ain't home yet." Her hair was rolled up in orange juice cans, and from the car I could hear them clinking.

"Rita," called Maxine, "this is my parents' house. I'm gonna park in the driveway." That's what I mean about style. Maxine and I said driveway, not yard, whether it was paved or not.

When we stepped out of the car, Rita yelled, "Jezum, what did you do to your hair?"

"Rita," said Maxine as if she was an Astor, "may I present my dear friend, Jo." Then she turned to me and said, gesturing back, "My sister-in-law, Rita."

"How do you do," I said in a tone befitting an officer's wife. Then we took our overnight bags into the house. Rita had a scornful look on her face. "Your old room is ready for you, Max, and your guest can have Becky's room."

"And where will Becky sleep?" asked Maxine.

"She's sleeping over at a friend's house." Rita walked into the kitchen. Maxine took our things upstairs and I followed Rita. The kitchen was dominated by a huge, black iron stove. My parents had one just like it until they modernized a few years back. The high point of this weekend was to be a supper party, but here it was late afternoon and not one thing was cooking. In fact, the stove wasn't even going.

"What can I do to help you, Rita?"

"Help me?"

"You know, get the supper ready. What can I do?"

"There is nothing to do. Folks will git here 'bout 5:30." She sat down at the drop-leaf table in the center of the room, folded her arms across her bosom, and pursed her lips as though she was trying not to say something.

Maxine walked into the room and said, "Too early for a little champagne, Rita?" She was carrying a bottle, wrapped in a plush bath towel for the long ride.

"You know I don't drink. That's your brother's department," said Rita in a less than friendly tone.

But, that didn't bother Maxine one bit. She opened the kitchen cabinet nearest the sink and took two glasses down from the top shelf. "Mum and Dad don't have flutes, but these crystal water goblets will do just fine." She pulled at the cork, and it blew up into the ceiling with such force that it left a little half moon in the plaster. The bubbles shot up, and champagne ran down the counter and onto the floor as Maxine, laughing, rushed to let it land in one of the goblets.

"Now, this place will smell like a brewery and everybody coming in a few hours," scolded Rita, grabbing a really big sponge from a soap dish on the sink. She blotted the counter and then the floor, intermittently wringing the sponge out over the sink.

"Rita, squeeze it into LaPetite's dish," said Maxine.

"Jezum, don't tell me that's LaPetite! How could you cut her hair like that and turn a perfectly good poodle pink? I am grateful your parents live in Florida. This would break their hearts," said Rita, wringing the sponge while kneeling on the floor.

"No, Rita, you are grateful they live in Florida so you and Pat can have this house all to yourselves. Cheers," said Maxine. clinking my glass.

I could see this was going to be a long couple of days. I wished we had gone to Boston.

Pat came downstairs after his shower with wet hair — what he still had of it. He was wearing a red undershirt and tan pants held up with plaid suspenders. I had asked Rita three times if I could at least set the table before her guests arrived. The last time she said, "My guests are bringing everything," so I just stopped asking. I wanted to remind her to go take her curlers out but didn't know how to bring up the topic. I gestured to Max once, making circular motions above my head. She gestured back making screw-ball circles around both her ears, and we fell into fits of laughter.

The doorbell rang and a couple entered. She was carrying a large stockpot, fastened with a bungee cord, and he had a loaf of bread in a plastic bag, swinging from the hand that carried a six pack. She set the pot on a cloth on the dining room table, ripped open the bread bag lengthwise and walked into the living room. She, too, had juice cans in her hair. Three more couples arrived and went through identical steps of leaving a pot on the table, tearing open some bread, and walking into separate rooms. The men were all in the kitchen with Maxine and me, where we were telling stories and polishing off the champagne. Every now and then, her brother would haul his suspenders out in front about a foot, let them snap against his chest and yell, "Ain't she a jeezer!" This could be about me or Max. All the guys, averaging in age from twenty to thirty, would yell back, "son-of-a-whore."

We hadn't noticed that the living room full of wives had gone silent until we heard all the juice cans clinking all at once. Rita walked into the kitchen and said, "Come an' git it." Then she walked to the dining room and pulled the light string over the table where a little army of pots sat flanked by Wonder bread. A pile of paper plates and plastic forks were at one end and some dilapidated brownies, still in the baking pan, at the other.

I whispered to Max, "I imagine this is how the army eats on bivouac."

"No," said Max, "this is Saturday suppah in the County."

I walked through the line three times, trying to find something I wanted to eat. I had never seen so many ways to fix baked beans: baked with slices of hot dogs, baked with pineapple, one in ruby-red sauce, another with broiled Spam wedges on the top, and one that looked so ordinary I didn't dare eat it. I ended up with a chunk of Velveeta cheese, a couple slices of Wonder bread, and a pile of pickles.

Pat said, "Trying to keep that figger of yers?"

"Yeah, sure," I said. "A person could starve at this party!"

"Ain't she a jeezer!" yelled Pat, and he snapped his suspenders with his thumb, tossing down a beer with the other hand.

The party ended at seven-thirty when the women came into the kitchen, carrying their pots and pans. Pat and Rita went to bed by eight. Max and I sat in the living room, looking at her family albums. We called her parents in Florida just before we went to bed at about ten.

I awakened the next morning to hear Rita shouting at Maxine in the next room. She was yelling about Maxine and I being in the kitchen with the men. "You take that goddamn pink dog and that jezebel, and you git out of my house!"

33

"Rita, this is my parents' house, remember?" said Max, still half asleep.

"Don't you ever darken my door agin," Rita barked. LaPetite joined right in as only poodles can. I sat up just as my door opened and Rita poked her head in. "I said git, and you I want out of town before folks start going to church."

"Are you going to church in the juice cans, Rita?" I asked.

"Yeah. Are you the church bell?" yelled Max from the hallway. "Where's my brother?"

"He's out moving your fancy car so you can git right on the road," she hissed and clinked off to the front bedroom, slamming the door.

"Just grab your stuff," said Maxine. "Rita is clearly a mental case. Toss on your clothes. We're out of here."

Pat was in the yard with a hangover bigger than the house. He said, "Sorry, Max. You know how Rita is —and — I have to live here." He barely lifted his eyes from his steel-toed boots.

"Boy! This beats all, Pat. Wait till I tell Mum and Daddy." Max pitched the overnight cases into the back. LaPetite peed on the tire and jumped into the front seat. We got in and backed out of the driveway.

"We should have gone to Boston," I said.

Five Children Under Five
- 1963 -

I offered to go to New Hampshire that August and babysit for my sister Tess and her husband so they could go to Cape Cod for a week. They hadn't had a vacation alone for five years. They had four children and I had one — all under the ages of five. Their home was a tiny, two-story frame house in a rural area of Manchester.

The first morning, the children paraded in to wake me, and I flew into action. I was prepared with a plan. I had set out all the outfits on the stairs in five little stacks; and I sat five little children on the appropriate steps, peeled off their pajamas and tossed them over the railing to the laundry room below. My great plan was I could contain the children there on the stairs so we would not have a reenactment of the three-ring circus staged last night, getting them ready for bed. I learned when you put five children in a bathtub, you should add water afterwards or be prepared for a flood. With them very clean but only half-clad in pajamas, they had scooted under furniture, jumped from bed to bed, and played toss-the-cats. By the time I got two of the cribs reassembled, I was in a state of collapse. So, lying in bed last night, I invented the stair-method-for-dressing-children. I put the wonderfully bright oldest child, my godson of four and a half, on the top step where he began to dress himself in earnest. Each step down got younger and more rambunctious.

"Aunt Jo, not my shirt," said Tim.

"It's OK, darling. Just pull it on. Here, I'll help you," I said, and his dark brown hair and matching eyes popped up through the neck hole of somebody else's polo shirt.

"Mikey doesn't want to wear that," said Jayne.

"It's OK, isn't it, Mikey?" I said as I stuffed his just-diapered lower body into large, red-plaid shorts.

They were like a pile of eels, squirming. Delighted with my lead, they began tossing clothes over the banister. I'd run down to retrieve what I needed and dash back up. I managed to get them all dressed in a very few minutes but not in the outfits I'd planned.

"It's OK, dear. You can wear a red sneaker and a blue one today because we are going to the woods."

Great cheers followed. The children marched down the stairs, holding on to the railing. There was a pile of clothes and towels from yesterday, plus the pajamas. It occurred to me that laundry would be a daily event. I thought, getting it hung on the clotheslines would require a plan.

I had Mikey on my hip as we headed to the kitchen, where I had set out (also during the middle of the night) five plastic bowls, four high chairs, and one step stool. I had papered the floor with the Sunday newspaper. To this day still, that meal remains a blur of milk spills, juice refills, towels, and children's voices at a decibel level near pain.

"Tim-Tim won't eat that," said Jayne, looking like a cherub and sounding very concerned. "He wants scrambled eggs, don't you, Tim-Tim?"

"That's nice, sweetheart, but Aunt Jo can only fix cereal this morning because we are all going to the woods." More cheers went up and more milk headed for the floor, filling a sneaker or two as it trailed by.

"Our mom cuts off crusts," said Joe, holding up his pale toast.

"Save them to take to the woods, honey," I said. "We might need them for a bear."

"Or a lion," shouted Joe, shoving the crusts into his pockets.

And my son, delighted to be in this exuberant pack, upended his cereal bowl on his head, laughing, and began slapping his hands in the milk as it dribbled onto the table. I just blotted him off with a towel and hoped the day wouldn't be hot enough to curdle him.

"Fucker! Fucker!" cried the baby. I stared at him, trying to imagine what he was trying to say.

"Mikey wants a cracker," said Tim. Two cats were licking up the milk while I wiped down all the toddlers with yet another towel, one more addition to the fast-mounting laundry.

"Woods! Woods!" yelled the children, and they began to leap into the air.

"Mikey peed," said Jayne.

"Don't open the door, sweethearts. Just get your helmets on while I change the baby."

"Fucker! Fucker!" said Mikey. I passed him two more crackers and laid him on the floor to change him as Jayne arrived to hand me a diaper.

"Now we go to the woods," cried Joe.

"Woods! Woods!" echoed my son and Tim.

"I want my blankie," said Jayne.

"Run and get it, sweetheart. We'll be in the backyard, sticking branches in our army helmets," I said, shoving the three little boys ahead of me while carrying Mikey, his fat fists gripping cracker mush. In a matter of minutes our bedraggled army was headed for the bivouac site. Jayne accompanied us, dragging a full-size, yellow blanket the color of her hair, sucking her thumb and humming Pomp and Circumstance. I could see their house from our encampment and had begged (yes, generals beg) the children to stay put (actually I had tied the baby between two trees so he could toddle between the trees but not travel very far) while I dashed back to the house to get a cup of tea. Holding on to my helmet, I flew as though the enemy had me in its scopes. Running hot tap water into a mug, I tried not to think what the inside of a water heater looks like. I tossed in a tea bag and had started to dash back, when I saw the big German cuckoo clock above the dripping table. It was 5:45 AM

New York City
– 1964 –

I try to erase New York City from my memory, but I still recall the promise it held. Perhaps I'd spent too much time in Leavitt's store, reading myself into the ink in the New Yorker . . . The Algonquin Hotel, Cheever, Dos Passos, Faulkner, cartoons of Booth cats and Thurber women.

The store was near our house on Main Street — oiled wooden floors, candy and fruit, and a huge magazine rack. Mr. Leavitt placed a wooden box near it for me, asking only that I handle the pages carefully. I was in high school and the world stretched out before me.

My marriage at nineteen was an escape from Bangor, Maine. And from years of sexual abuse by a priest, unknown to anyone. I worked after school six days a week at the priest house. My job was to answer the doorbell and phone. My life at the priest house suddenly changed when the young priest arrived. It was as if I was very close to a jack-in-the-box. The priest would pop into the pantry and touch me all over, or pop out of a corridor and embrace me passionately, or turn off the light on the sun porch and kiss me so wildly my lips swelled. I would never have let a boy my age do any of these things, but this was different. It was terrifying and thrilling all in one moment. I can't explain it. The priest told me if I didn't tell anyone, it wasn't a sin. He said he wanted to marry me.

Then one evening I opened the front door of the priest house and a young, and beautiful-like-a-movie-star woman was standing there, enveloped in the scent of summer flowers. She said she had an appointment with the young priest. I showed her to the office and buzzed for father. He dashed down the stairs and into the office. He shut off the light.

I didn't know what to think, but I sensed that Father Jack-in-the-Box would never marry me. It became too much to bear. I feared God would never forgive me.

One night at the priest house I fell to the kitchen floor. My legs were paralyzed. I bumped my head but the pain was in my legs. I lay there past my work time. I was responsible for turning off the lights on the sun porch, kitchen and back hallways. When one of the priests came in, he must have noticed all the lights were on. I tried to get up but couldn't. I called out to him. I remember he asked if he should call the doctor, but I insisted I'd be fine. "Would you please take me home, Father." He said, "Of course. Are you going to be all right?" He lifted me up and carried me to the Monsignor's green Oldsmobile. He placed me in the back seat, which smelled faintly of leather and cigars.

My parents were shocked to open the door and see one of the priests standing there, carrying me in his arms. I don't know what was said. I was trying to crawl inside myself where despair was waiting.

The doctor did come. He sounded like he was speaking underwater and told them I was in shock. I couldn't eat and barely drank. A terrible weakness came over me. My parents sent for Tess to come home from nursing school in Portland to help Mum, who could not stop crying. I wanted to tell her I'd be all right, but she seemed so far away.

Then Tess was sitting close to the bed. She was talking sternly as a nun. "Don't you dare die! Now open your mouth. Suck on this ice chip," she said as she forced the cold slivers between my lips. She was sitting there every time I opened my eyes. Soon she was speaking sweetly and Mum was standing there, not crying. They helped me walk to the bathroom and to a chair by the bay window. Tess saved my life. She returned to nursing school and had to make up the two weeks in order to receive her diploma.

I was still filled with the hope of finding a happy life. I was wrong. My life was filled with martinis and a hapless marriage to an Air Force officer. And then we had a beautiful son. We moved to a butte in South Dakota. My husband was surprisingly incompetent and drunk most of the time. I was certain there was a better life, a better way to raise our son. I needed a plan.

I hurried back to Bangor and my parents' home, my son in tow. Only my sister Annie was happy to see us. When my father came home each night from his barbershop, I heard myself call out, "Hi, Daddy. Did you have a nice day?"

His reply was always the same: "When are you leaving!" I became numb to his remarks until I heard him say to Mum, "We don't have divorce in our family." I was ashamed and frightened.

The priest appeared, and then disappeared. Once it was a surprise visit when I was babysitting my son and two small children in a cabin at Holbrook Pond near Bangor. Sometimes it was a phone call where he didn't speak. If he was God's presence on earth, what did this mean?

Within a few weeks, Annie took my son and me to catch the Greyhound bus for Cape Cod. I was sure I could find a job there and a place for us to live. In the course of one day, I found us a family to live with and a job as a waitress. The family's housekeeper would take care of my son evenings while I worked. I didn't have a car anymore, so I hitchhiked. This was a new experience, a bit scary, but pretty common on the Cape in summertime. I made a plan. I worked a lot, slept very little, and except for paying room and board, I hoarded wages and tips. This money and the promised child support would get us to New York City.

Then one day I moved to New York City with my young son. But the great life in the city was eluding me. I was losing confidence and fear nudged against me. I had been here two months and had interviewed for eleven jobs. Yesterday, when the child support check did not arrive, I went to a welfare office in Midtown. Sitting there in that noisy place, I told the woman I was in temporary financial difficulty.

She interrupted me. "Name?"

I told her. "Address?" She didn't even write it down, just looked at me and said, "We don't send welfare to people who live on East 57th Street! Why are you here?"

I told her again that the child support payment was two months behind, and I wanted to see if I could borrow rent money because I didn't have a job yet. She looked me straight in the eyes from behind long, straight bangs and said, "This ain't a bank. You in a lot of trouble, girl. Next?" I wanted to tell her this was temporary, plead my case, appeal to her to help me. She beckoned to the woman behind me.

It hadn't occurred to me that I wouldn't succeed. I walked all the way back to the apartment — the apartment with cushions on the floor next to lamps without their tables. I couldn't afford to have the couch and big furnishings hoisted up to the sixth floor. The bedroom was all set up for my son — leopard bedspread, fur throw rug, telescope, and bureau. I slept in the living room on the cushions on the floor.

Today I had an interview at a representative firm right on Fifth Avenue, next door to the gem-like Tiffany building. A rep firm is the conduit between ad agencies and TV stations all across the country. I had applied at all the television and radio stations but to no avail. This application was lengthy.

When I came to the question about job experience, I wasn't sure what to write. I had only had one job after high school in a television station in Bangor, doing traffic. I even got to be the traffic manager after one year because the other two women quit! But this was New York City, and I had three dollars and ten cents left in the world.

I needed this job but couldn't imagine what to say to make them hire me. I wrote TV Traffic Manager on the application and handed it to the receptionist. She glanced at it and immediately dialed a short number. She stared at me the whole time and said, "Marjorie, there is an applicant here for that opening in your department. Her experience is TV traffic!" She hung up and said, "Marjorie will be right out." It seemed to me that most places where I applied for a job had supervisory women named Marjorie. Was it the female equivalent of Major?

Marjorie came around the receptionist's desk and asked me to follow her. She was a tall, harried-looking woman and asked several questions about my experience. She seemed interested in my one-and-only job: I had broken out the Nielsen and Arbitron rating books, applied the stats and demographics to my traffic boards, and calculated cost per thousand in the desired demo. She explained that this job was to do exactly that, and coordinate orders and cancellations between their New York office and client TV stations. The opening was for a coordinator for Kansas City, Atlanta, and Philadelphia who could break out the ratings within one business day. It was just like my job in Bangor, Maine! These were just larger markets. Then Marjorie leaned forward, removed her glasses, and asked, "When would you be available?"

"Monday," I said without hesitation. It was Friday.

She smiled a tired smile and said she would be in touch. All eleven interviews had ended this way.

When I got to the apartment, I explained to the sitter, Emma, that I was still looking for a job and that she shouldn't be discouraged. I told her I didn't have the money to pay her then, but I surely would next week.

"Then I'm taking the chicken," she said, pointing at the package thawing on the kitchen counter.

"Let's share it, Emma," I replied, trying not to sound desperate.

She put the entire package in her handbag. "I'll also be taking two dresses," she said and opened the hall closet. She took out my favorite cocktail dress, black with a low-cut back. I had high hopes that I would have an occasion to wear it in New York, perhaps to The Algonquin. Then she took a blue striped shirtdress. She stuffed these in her purse, too. I wanted to say they wouldn't fit her, she was twice my size, but then I realized she was planning to sell them. She needed a paycheck, too.

My son came bounding into the room, dressed in his pinto-like pony chaps and cowboy hat, playing the part of his TV hero, Roy Rogers. "Howdy, Dale," he said.

"Howdy, Roy," I replied as Emma slammed the door. "Let's go for a walk." It was not yet dark. A gusty breeze met us as we turned on Second Avenue and walked to Sutton Place. I zipped my son's jacket, pulled up the hood, and let the cowboy hat ride between his shoulders like a backpack. There was a charming park there where we would see governesses wheeling their charges around in prams. They were not there this late in the day.

I was engulfed in despair. I had put my precious boy in harm's way. We were both in peril. I thought about the three dollars and ten cents — all that separated us from homelessness. In a late-night call to my mother I had asked if I could come home. I heard Dad's voice in the background. "Tell her she made her bed. Now she can lie in it." I could tell Mum was crying and I was, too. "Dad said no, dear." Divorce was "against our religion." I knew that, but I didn't know what to do. Perhaps God had left me to my sins. I was terrified.

I walked my cowboy to the little park above the East River. My sweet boy was talking to me the whole way, and somehow I answered. My fear shoved me forward, over uneven sidewalks. An ambulance screamed by, followed closely by an off-duty cab. Had I been courageous to come to this huge city or naive? What was going to happen to us!

Behind us, lights were beginning to glow in the Sutton Place multi-million-dollar co-ops. In front, the East River's slate color echoed the gray sky. The current was swift and should carry us quickly. There are few places to climb out, or for rescue. The danger was not in jumping. It was that we'd be separated. I could not bear that pain, but I couldn't decide how we could both scale the high railing and land in the river together. I knelt down and hugged him to me. I picked him up and pressed him against the railing. How could I not kill us? I had broken more than one Commandment. He was perplexed at my weeping and asked, "Why are you crying, Mommy?"

Coldness crept over my skin. The only warmth was from my son's little arms, encircling my neck. He was patting me, comforting me, as if I had fallen down. I could see the 59th Street Bridge with shadowy headlights and taillights endlessly crossing. With all the courage I could summon I said, "I was just thinking that we should walk to the park, and you could have a pony ride. I have ten cents right here." It was a long walk for little five-year-old legs, but we stopped and looked at window displays. Our favorite was FAO Schwarz with their window full of bears! And then we were at the park. I bought the ticket. The attendant lifted him up on the pony, and he went round and round, my little cowboy, waving each time he passed by me. It was late by then, and we walked back to the apartment. I decided we would have pancakes for supper. Cowboys love pancakes.

As soon we entered the apartment, I saw the red light blinking on the answering machine. I pushed down on the button, "Hello, Jo. This is Marjorie. We were all very pleased with your credentials. The job is yours. I'll see you on Monday at 9 o'clock. You can call me at home tonight with any questions." She left her number.

I played the message again. Roy Rogers and Dale Evans jumped up and down on the couch cushions. I thanked God. I promised my son three storybooks at bedtime.

The Value House
– 1969 –

I'd done everything imaginable to assure the success of this
meeting with a prospective advertiser. About a month earlier, the
TV station in Bangor where I worked (yes, again, but this time not
in traffic) had received a letter duplicated by mimeograph asking for
suggestions for a grand opening. The other salesmen didn't think it
was a likely advertiser because of the Lewiston address (two hours
south and outside our TV signal area) so I asked for the lead. The
company name was Benson & Sullivan, a tobacco wholesaler, and it
was signed by a Mr. Charles E. Day. I called the phone number but
never did reach Mr. Day. On one of these calls, I asked why were they
coming to Bangor. To open a smoke shop? The man named Dana said
they were coming to open a catalog showroom, The Value House. I
asked where I could get a catalog and was told that Mr. Day's uncle
had an accounting firm in Bangor and would probably lend me his
copy. I picked it up and was delighted to see the range of merchandise
and the low prices. That is when I made the plan.

I wrote to the major vendors, General Electric, Panasonic,
Sunbeam, Zenith and the like, and asked for copies of TV commercials
for a grand opening. I also asked if they offered any cooperative funds
for TV advertising. To my surprise, most did! At this time there was
actually a push by our power company to help pay for advertising
for anything that plugged in. So I wrote to them and got more co-op
dollars. What I didn't know was the size of the grand opening budget.
So I called Dana again, but he didn't know. He suggested I make a
recommendation.

Oh, one other thing I learned from the uncle was that Mr. Day was an investor in another TV channel in Bangor. I needed a very good plan.

I carefully typed and retyped the grand opening proposal, listing all major vendors from whom I had secured co-op funds. I also showed how much money the power company would kick in. So the $5,000 budget I was proposing was more than doubled with matching funds. I wrote all this up at night, after my son was asleep, and the housekeeper with the chipped glass eye was in her room. I was not allowed to use the sales secretary at work. Perhaps the assumption was if you're a girl you should know how to type. I rented a typewriter, preferring to do proposals at home. The last page was a multiple-choice form for Mr. Day. I wondered if he would choose DON'T YOU KNOW I OWN STOCK IN A COMPETITIVE STATION? Or DOUBLE THE BUDGET!

I drove all the way to my Lewiston appointment in my unsafe-at-any-speed Corvair. It was a convertible, but the heater was stuck in the on position so it worked out pretty well on average. Dana met me in the office lobby. He was not as tall as he seemed on the telephone. He said, "Mr. Day isn't available…he's tied up in a meeting." I masked my disappointment and said I had a proposal for Mr. Day. Dana smiled and answered, "I will be sure it is on his desk as soon as possible. I'll call you when I know what date he is coming to Bangor."

On the drive back to Bangor, I contemplated the wisdom of the four-hour-round-trip drive. My boss did not pay mileage. I sure hoped there was a chance I would get some advertising dollars.

The very next day Dana called. "We will be in Bangor next Thursday. Mr. Day would like to meet with you. Do you want him to come to the station?"

"No, ask him to meet me at the Pilot's Grill around noon for lunch. We can discuss the grand opening then." I was really excited. After all, no one makes an appointment not to buy. Right?

The Pilot's Grill was a family-owned restaurant near the end of the huge military base runway. Before the area was built up, you could dine and watch fighter planes and refueling jets take off and land. Mr. Zodias, the present owner, knew my dad. I drove out there that very day and told Mr. Zodias about my important business meeting. I showed him the small table I wanted, just inside the lounge. I said, "Please do not bring the bill. I will come back later to pay you."

He looked a bit concerned, perhaps because he knew my boss did not pay expenses. "How many people?" he asked.

"Just the two," I said, trying to instill confidence in Mr. Zodias.

"What time?"

"I expect my client to arrive around noon. I'll arrive a bit earlier. OK?"

Mr. Zodias seemed pleased that I had become a businesswoman. He smiled graciously and said, "See you Thursday at noon. Say hello to your dad."

The day arrived sunny and clear. I went to the Pilot's Grill a bit before noon. And, as if rehearsed, Mr. Zodias greeted me with a slight bowing gesture and said, "Your table is ready."

I sat down, took out a copy of the proposal, and placed it in the center of the table. Time seemed to stand still. I looked at my watch frequently. Mr. Zodias had popped his head around the divider twice, asking if I wanted a beverage. Each time I politely declined, adding, "I'll wait for my client." It was now 12:30. There were only a few other people in the lounge having lunch.

Suddenly there was a great clatter of voices, and Mr. Zodias said, "Your party is here." Six men charged into the room. Fighter jets flew over. It sounded like the entire squadron. Mr. Zodias pulled over another table, a large one.

One of the men was Dana, and I was trying to decide which one was Mr. Day when he extended his hand and said, "I'm Charlie Day." He was medium height, wore an elegantly dark, tailored suit yet had a disheveled air about him. He had on a glistening-white, monogrammed shirt with a loosened silk tie. Mostly he seemed restless, except for his eyes. They were dark brown, filled with kindness and a kind of merriment. He sat down next to me and told me about the store. Discounting was a fairly rare practice at that time so I was fascinated. "The two most important things are: I should be able to charge any price I want, and people should know I'll guarantee every product. If it isn't satisfactory, bring it back. Starting with this store, our third one, we are breaking Fair Trade. It's price fixing, not fair at all." He picked up the menu.

I was amazed to hear all this and wanted to be part of it. "Won't you get hauled into court?" I asked.

"I'm looking forward to it." And I saw that his smile was not just merriment – it was mischief! He pulled his glasses down from the top of his head and said, "What's good for lunch?"

"I recommend the grilled cheese and tomato open sandwich. It's terrific!" I said this with great exuberance while mentally multiplying by seven. I talked to calm myself — it will be OK. That was before they all ordered cocktails. Mr. Zodias delivered these himself. He gave me a look that seemed to convey, "Remember, you are coming back to pay for this."

Since Mr. Day asked me to order first, I said, "I'd like the grilled cheese and tomato open sandwich, please."

Then they ordered lunch: lobster dinners, a t-bone steak, and one man ordered sole meuniére! It took two waiters to deliver the food.

Mr. Day turned to me and said, "That's quite a proposal. Great job. Double the budget to $10,000 and line up all the co-op dollars you can."

"Do you have an opening date?" I asked.

"I'll know today when I see the progress on the renovations."

Mr. Zodias came around the corner, and I tried my best to give him the OK sign. I wanted to assure him I could afford this lunch. I gave him a wink. He looked horrified. Then the men jumped up, and Mr. Day said he'd ride with me to the store location under construction in a former bowling alley, near the Broadway Shopping Center. We both stood up, and Mr. Day said, "I need the check."

"It's all taken care of, Mr. Day. My treat."

"No, really. I want the check."

I smiled and said, "I've taken care of the check."

Mr. Day made a fist and hit the table, setting silverware, cups and saucers clattering. He yelled, "BRING ME THE CHECK!"

I called out, "BRING HIM THE CHECK."

Mr. Zodias appeared as if by hovercraft and said, "THE CHECK."

Mr. Day tossed a pile of bills on the table, and we headed to my Corvair. Dana and the entourage drove by us in a big, green Lincoln.

The White Dinner
- 1980 -

When I heard their car on the gravel driveway, I struck a match to the firewood and pushed the play button on the stereo. The Ink Spots sang, "You always hurt the ones you love..." The doorbell chimed, and my two friends walked into the living room.

"Hi, Toots," said Tom.

"Hi, guys," I answered.

"Jo, don't even talk to me until he has a drink," Mark said, as he exhaled what was more like a sigh. I met Mark at Goddard College in the late sixties, where he was studying the Tao of Herb Gardening, and we'd been friends ever since.

"Thanks for wearing white," I said, pouring three glasses of white wine.

"I feel like the Pillsbury Doughboy," said Mark. He did look a little like the Pillsbury Doughboy, but a very tall, handsome doughboy. Tom, on the other hand, looked as if he had been abandoned in his confirmation suit so long ago that he had grown a mustache. Mark collapsed onto the couch, which slid back into the wall. His feet flew forward, kicking the top of the glass coffee table, and the wine bottle fell to the floor. Its contents spun out on the polished hardwood.

"No problem," I said with great reserve, mopping it up with the white damask napkins.

"It will be a problem if you don't have more," groaned Mark.

"Never mind, Toots. I'll drink his glass and mine."

Mark, still draped over the couch, said, "We brought you one of our new line of wastebaskets." For ten years they had been marketing their artwork: trompe l'oeil furniture, wall murals, faux blueberry pies — all with a touch of humor. I'd collected quite a few pieces. My favorites were my living room floor lamp with papier-mâché morning glories climbing up from the base and the purple-and-gold-striped puffer fish dangling on a length of filament from the ceiling in my bathroom. I had seen the wastebaskets last month in their gallery and coveted one.

"We call these wastebaskets the neo-Laura Ashley line," chirped Tom, tossing down his glass of wine and blotting his mustache on the back of his hand.

Mark continued, "It's still in the car. I can't touch another wastebasket today, at least not on an empty stomach." He looked exhausted.

I asked, "Have you filled the Horchow order yet?"

"We fill it and fill it and fill it!" said Tom. "Did we tell you he forgot to include shipping costs in our price quote? We're going to make about three cents on each wastebasket."

"Shut up, Tom," Mark said, rather flatly. "Jo, he has not stopped talking once on the hour-long drive here. Can we just eat and not talk about wastebaskets or Horchow?"

"Sure," I said. "Just give me a minute." I walked through the arch to the dining room. I could still smell the starch on the freshly ironed white linens. I lit the candles and the candelabra shimmered. So did the silverware. Down the center of the table I had scattered white rose petals. No detail would be lost on my friends. Perfect.

I stepped into the kitchen and called my daughter-in-law, Hannah. I asked her to drop off a nice bottle of white wine on her way home from work. Then I arranged the dinner on the white china plates: white asparagus, poached chicken, tiny boiled new potatoes and a sprig of green grapes. I sprinkled freshly chopped cilantro on top like confetti, then carried these to the dining room on a silver tray.

Catching a glimpse of myself in the hall mirror, I smoothed my long white dress — not an Emily Dickinson bride-like dress, but an Ingrid Bergman Casa Blanca dress. I picked up my crystal bell and the clapper clinked. Mark and Tom came right in.

"Shades of Bergdorf Goodman!" said Tom. "This looks like one of my window displays." I often like to time how long into a visit it takes Tom to mention Bergdorf's. Usually it's under an hour. That night it was thirty-five minutes.

"How beautiful!" said Mark, sitting down. "I wasn't sure what you meant by a white dinner." They had been working nonstop for two weeks, and I thought this dinner would be a nice break. "Well," he said, looking around, "the wastebasket we brought you isn't white."

"Neither are the Ink Spots," said Tom, patting his mustache. "This looks elegant, Toots. I suppose you're going to say that you just threw it together?"

"Tom, give it a rest," Mark groaned.

Tom sat at the head of the table with two empty wineglasses.

Placing the dinners in front of them, I sat down and gazed around the room. It looked perfect.

Tom cut into his chicken. "Hell! It's alive!" Pink juice squirted out of the raw center.

I was horrified. How could this have happened! I reached across the table, picked the chicken breasts up in my bare hands, tossed them on the tray, and said, "Oh, gods! I'll be right back." I dashed into the kitchen and tossed the chicken into the stockpot, turning the heat on high. I did square breathing, drawing in a large breath, holding it, then exhaling from my toes.

The music followed me into the kitchen. "I want to buy a paper doll that I can call my own..." The back door opened. Hannah came in with a large paper bag balanced on a tiny hip. She was wearing a pink linen dress and had tied her long auburn hair to one side. "Is Sauterne OK?" she asked.

My mind did a back flip. I hoped my eyes were not betraying my dismay. "Thanks, darling, it will be fine," I heard myself saying in a calm voice.

"Hey, Toots, is that the wine?" called Tom.

I shut off the stove. "Meet me out front, guys," I yelled, "and bring the candelabra." I walked out the back door, carrying the bag with the wine. As my daughter-in-law drove off, I took my new floral wastebasket out of Mark's gray Chevy wagon. I sat down on the curbstone and upended the wastebasket in front of me. The guys came out the front door, walked right over to where I was sitting, placed the candelabra on top of the wastebasket and sat down. I unscrewed the bottle, twisted the bag around the neck, took a big swig and passed it to Mark, who passed it to Tom.

"I knew I was in for a treat," said Tom, taking a pull and passing the bag back to me.

"You never fail to surprise us, Jo," said Mark. "What did you call that chicken dish?"

"Chicken al Dente," I said, taking another gulp and spilling some of it on my white dress. It was just getting dark. Cars were driving along Main Street, slowing down, then driving on. The music drifted out the front door. I began to sing along and Tom joined in. "You're nobody 'til somebody loves you..."

The Tree Lighting
- 1986 -

The tree lighting in Monument Square is an annual tradition just after sunset on the Saturday following Thanksgiving. I bundled up my three-year-old grandson, Jeramy, in a snowsuit, knit cap and thermal boots, and we headed out at dusk. There was an icy wind off the bay, swirling snow across the brick sidewalks on Commercial Street. It nudged us along as we hurried toward the square. Quite a crowd had already assembled, and they were singing Christmas carols. "God rest ye, merry gentlemen, let nothing you dismay…"

I lifted Jeramy up to stand on a large granite planter so that he could see above the crowd. The tree was an enormous spruce, some fifty feet tall, and secured with cables against Portland's winter winds. The mayor was to throw the switch at an appointed moment, and a city maintenance worker was working feverishly at the mechanism.

Night descended. A large cutout of a moon rose above the Eastern Promenade. People were stamping their feet to keep warm. Scarves were retied to cover cold faces, yet puffs of steamy breath escaped. After a rousing chorus of "Jingle Bells," the crowd fell quiet. There was clearly an impatient restlessness.

Suddenly, out of nowhere, there was a group of five people carrying a white banner and snaking silently through the crowd. A tall man in a long coat and red earmuffs was carrying the front edge of the banner. He seemed to be as surprised to see us as we were to see them. I caught a glimpse of the words painted there in black block letters: FREE TIBET. RETURN THE DALI LAMA. People began to murmur.

"What's it say?" someone called out from behind us.

My grandson turned, and yelled back, "It says Hurry up and light the tree." The crowd applauded, and the mayor pulled the switch. Someone began to sing, "We wish you a Merry Christmas," and the crowd joined in.

My grandson and I hurried down the hill on that crisp, cold night, back to my condo and a bowl of warm soup. That night I told him the story of Bethlehem again. Someday soon I would tell him the story of a place north of the Himalayas.

Finding Her
- 1987 -

We had nearly finished setting the table. My granddaughter Marcie, age six and a half, was folding the floral napkins in pleats, our favorite way.

"Mama and Lenny are gonna love this party," she said, placing the napkins in the stemmed glasses where they posed like birds in flight. Then she opened the tiny parasols and placed them at the base of the glasses. "Oh, Grammy, these are such cute umbrellas! I'm givin' you the pink one, yellow for me. Mama and Lenny git blue and green!"

I was getting the tray ready. Watching her through the archway in the kitchen, I remembered how I had avoided any contact with her or her mother for nearly five years. Her mother was only a teenager, and my son was married to someone else when she was born. My son said if I contacted Marcie I would never see him again. Then my son disappeared from my life, and I hastened to find her. Now the third weekend of every month finds me driving an hour north of Portland to pick her up.

The first time she came to spend the night I was apprehensive. We had only had day trips before, and I was concerned that she would miss her mother and want to go home. When I expressed this to her mother, she had said, "Marcie'd go anywhere with you. All she talks about is sleeping over at your house."

The following month I arranged the overnight. When we arrived at the condo, she raced down the hallway and into the living room, stopping with both her arms raised, like a school crossing guard. "Hey," she had said. "Is this your house or is this a store?"

59

Now I couldn't imagine my life without her—this constant-motion machine of a girl who spent part of each weekend lining up my collections of frogs and dragon figurines, struggling to read and trying to tell the time. I looked in at her as she put a blue wooden frog in the middle of the table, and I said, "The table looks beautiful, sweetie-pie. Come check with me to see if I have everything ready for the breakfast sundaes."

She skipped into the kitchen. "Oh, oh, Grammy. Lenny don't like granola," she said.

"That's OK, sweetie. There are plenty of good things he can put on his sundae—strawberries, blueberries, coconut, raisins..." Lenny was the mother's live-in boyfriend. He had a meanness about him that he carried coiled up in his barrel-like stance. Often, when I came to pick Marcie up, he would stand backward in their kitchen as if I couldn't see him. I would make it a point to walk over and say hello just to see him stomp off into the adjoining room. One time as we were leaving and Marcie was saying her good-byes, she had said, "Good-by, Mr. Stick."

"Who is Mr. Stick?" I asked.

"That's him, there," she said and pointed to a large branch by the kitchen stove. "If the dog is bad, Mr. Stick hits 'im. And if I am bad, Lenny has Mr. Stick hit me," she said.

"Perhaps Mr. Stick needs to disappear in Portland," I replied.

Marcie dashed across the room and brought the branch to me. "Here, Grammy," she had said, letting go of it as if it were hot. When we got to my car, I snapped Mr. Stick in half with the heel of my shoe and tossed him into the trunk. Then I looked up and saw Lenny watching from the kitchen window. That night I called the mother and told her she must not allow Lenny to hit Marcie. "You don't know how bad she is," she said. That was earlier that spring.

"Where's the yogurt?" asked Marcie, hopping on one foot, swinging her long blond hair. "Did you get French vanilla?"

"I sure did, but I'll leave it in the fridge until your mother gets here."

"Can I go out on the balcony?" she asked.

"Yes, sweetie-blue-eyes."

"Bye."

She skipped through the dining room, and I heard the glass slider open to the balcony and the screen close behind her. I pushed the tray to the back of the counter and went to join her. We loved to sit at the little wrought-iron table on the balcony and look back at the tall city buildings, mostly banks. Pink flamingos, wearing our handmade, beaded necklaces, peered out of the flower boxes. I stepped out on the balcony. She was not there.

"Marcie? Marcie!" I called out, not yet in a panic but feeling it rise in my throat. "Sweetie" I called, looking up the slanted roof. Then I dared to look over the railing to the parking lot below. She was not to be seen. I could barely breathe and a pressure began to expand inside my head. "Marcie! Marcie! Where are you?" I cried and dashed back into the condo. I flew up the ladder from the living room to the sleeping loft. She wasn't there. I dashed down and checked the bathroom and the little library. Something in my neck joined the pounding in my head, and I started praying out loud, blubbering, "Angel of God, angel of God"... I couldn't think of a proper prayer. Then I saw two little pink sneakers protruding from the back of the gold couch.

"Oh, my God!" I screamed when I saw her lying there, eyes fixed wide open. I picked her up.

She said, "Hi, Grammy."

My terror melted into relief. "Oh, sweetie! Don't ever do this to Grammy!" I burst into tears.

"Why are you bawlin'?" she asked.

"I was so frightened something bad had happened to you."

The intercom rang. "I'll git it," Marcie said and ran to the hallway to buzz our guests in.

"Sorry we're late," said the mother. "Me and Lenny played bingo late and over-slept." I was in the kitchen blowing my nose, trying to compose myself. I stepped out to greet them. Marcie was trying to scramble up her mother's long, blue-jean-clad legs. "Git off me," her mother said. "You're too big fer me to hold." The mother pushed her long brown hair back from her face only to have it tumble back down. Lenny scuffed his work boots back and forth on the carpet and kept his eyes there. They declined taking off their jackets.

Marcie said, "The party is ready, Mama. Come see how pretty. Me and Grammy made it." All the while she was pulling on her mother's sleeve.

I said, "Please come in and sit down." I got out the compote of yogurt and put it and the silver tray on the buffet.

Marcie slipped into her place at the table. "Mama, sit there. And Lenny, you sit across from Grammy." She waited until they sat down. "First you take your napkin out and put it on your lap. I folded 'em myself."

Lenny snapped, "You don't do that at home."

"We ain't got no napkins."

Her mother said, "D'ya set the table, too?"

"Yup."

Lenny said a bit louder, "You don't do that at home either!" He shot the mother a hot look, and she turned to Marcie as if he hadn't spoken.

Marcie took her napkin from her glass and said, "We call these breakfast sundaes. Now, you do everything I do. OK?"

"We already ate," the mother said.

"But, we made the party for you," Marcie said, her lips moving as if she was chewing.

"I'll eat with you," I said. And so we began our ritual, making our favorite concoction, layering the yogurt and fruit, and sprinkling the granola on the top.

Lenny blurted, "When d'ya start eatin' yogurt?"

"Grammy gits the one I like," Marcie said. "And she has these spoons." She held up her favorite silver spoon by its carved rosebud handle.

"Why don't you act good at home?" asked Lenny. Then he just sat there, watching us eat, his arms folded across his chest, still wearing his Valvoline baseball cap.

The mother said, "Maybe you'll be good for us when we git you home."

Marcie put her arms out to the side, palms raised, head forward and said, "My Grammy says I'm the best girl in Portland. Ain't I, Grammy?"

Lenny hissed, "Ain't ain't a word!" Then he looked down at the sleeves of his jacket as if they were not his.

Marcie dropped her hands to the table. "Ain't it, Grammy?"

"It's not a word we like as much as the words breakfast sundaes," I said softly, smiling through the troubled air crowding in around us.

Marcie and I finished eating, and then it was time for them to go. The mother and Lenny headed for the hallway. I turned around for Marcie. She was nowhere to be seen. "Did Marcie go ahead to get the elevator?" I asked.

"Ain't she with you?" asked the mother, peering around me.

"She's hiding," Lenny said. "That's her new thing. Makes me Christly crazy." He yanked on the brim of his cap. "We're leaving her!"

"Marcie, you git out here," yelled her mother.

"We're leavin' you!" hollered Lenny.

I said, "Go ahead down to the truck. I'll bring her down."

The door slammed behind them. I rushed to the gold couch and looked over the back. There she was, lying flat on her back with her eyes squinted shut. "Come, sweetie-pie. Grammy will carry you. It's time to go home." I lifted the tall, lanky child. Her legs curled around my waist and hung halfway down my legs. She nestled her blond head on my shoulder and wrapped her arms around my back.

"I hate you, Grammy," she whispered.

"I know, sweetie," I said softly against her ear. "I know."

I carried her to the elevator.

Migrations

- 1989 -

It was a cold Friday in February. I called her in the late afternoon. The phone rang once. "Hello," she said tentatively.

"Hi, Mummy. It's Jo."

"Oh, darlin'! Where are you calling from?"

"Portland," I said.

"What in the world are you doing way down there?"

"I live here now, Mummy." My calls to her always started this way. I'd moved to Portland five years earlier. "I'm coming up tomorrow," I said, "and I was wondering what you would like to do."

"Oh, I don't know, darlin'," she said. Then added quickly, "I need some new panty hose."

"I'll bring you some, Mummy," I said. I made a note to go by the house and pick some up. She had joined a panty hose club, and one drawer of her bureau and a half one of Dad's were filled with little cello-packs, all beige-tone with control top. Not a sandal foot among them. "What else do you need?" I asked.

"Well, dear," she whispered, "I don't have any underpanties."

"Eileen!" I exclaimed. "Are you bare-ass in Orono?"

"Merciful God, no!" she shot back. "I have one pair on. The pink ones are hanging up in the bathroom." She began to whisper again, "That's all I have, two pair."

"Then we'll go buy some new ones," I said. "Now, I plan to wash all your sweaters for you. Set them out in your rocking chair. I'll pick them up in the morning."

"I'll do it right now," she said. The telephone clunking down on her nightstand was an explosion in my ear. I could hear her opening and closing drawers. I could hear her pulling sweaters off the chrome hangers permanently attached to the closet clothes bar. The cuffs of all the sweaters would be smudged with printer's ink from the Bangor Daily News, which our older sister Tess arranged to be delivered to her room. Mum was always delighted when it arrived. "The paper is here!" she would say, and opening it flat on her bed, she would read what interested her. Then she would fold it up exactly as it had arrived and set it aside. Minutes later she would exclaim, "The paper is here!" and begin the process all over again.

I could hear her footsteps slapping back and forth against the asphalt tile. Finally she picked up the phone. "There are four, dear. I put them on my rocker. The cuffs are disgraceful. Can you do four?"

"Sure can," I said. "I'll do them by hand at Annie's. I'll use the Eileen LaFlamme out damn spot method."

"Darn spot, dear, darn." Mum could get any kind of spot out of any kind of fabric.

"It occurred to me, Mummy, that we did not do the fall cleaning," I said. "Shall we do that tomorrow when we come to see you?"

"Oh, darlin', that would be wonderful, she said. Cleaning was her passion. "Do you have cleaning rags?"

"We'll bring plenty," I said. "I thought we'd do the bureau, the nightstand, maybe the closet? Then you can decide what else needs to be done."

"Yes, sweetheart. I'll see you tomorrow," she said.

The drive up I-95 that night to my sister Annie's home took two hours under a clear sky, with snow brightening the edges of the road and covering the fields. Last night's snow clung to the north side of the trees. As I drove, my thoughts drifted to Mum. Was it a blessing, her forgetting that Dad had died? Or that he had ever lived? Did she long for the snug little ranch house with the gardens and all the bird feeders in the back? Or had that, too, slipped away.

"It's a non-Alzheimer's brain disease," the specialist at the Alzheimer's Clinic in Waterville had said. "Alzheimer's is like a down escalator. It pretty much progresses on schedule. Your mother's brain disease is different. She may go down a few steps, then pause, then descend more rapidly. Nothing new can be introduced. And I don't recommend letting her live alone."

Because of this diagnosis we took out the microwave oven, got sensors for the electric stove burners and hung up old pictures. We got her a cat, which she kept tossing into the yard. "If you know what's good for you, Mister Kitty, you'll go home where you belong."

Shortly after that, my nephew Scott moved in with Mum and her condition became more apparent. Each morning when he came out to the kitchen, Mother would look up in astonishment, not remembering why he was there. Once the smoke alarm went off, and he found himself running to the kitchen to carry a burning pan of chicken out to the backyard. One evening she opened the door to the den while he was taping an assignment for one of his broadcasting school classes.

"Why are you touching Grampie's things?" she had cried. "He is going to be angry when he gets home, young man." Later, when he played the tape back for us, the microphone had recorded her anxiety.

Soon after that, Annie and her husband took over Mum's daily care and brought her home with them for supper every night. Still, her confusion grew. Sometimes, when they arrived to pick her up, she would be sitting at the maple kitchen table, eating her breakfast, a bowl of shredded wheat, unable to fathom why they were there. One Saturday, a year and a half ago, she collapsed in the backseat while

Annie and I were driving her to the supermarket. She was taken to the hospital and, while she was there, suffered a series of mini-strokes and never got to go home again.

Now the car radio began to crackle as I drove beyond the station's range. I shut it off, leaning forward to observe how the low moon appeared to be racing along beside me, darting behind the tall, black pines. I thought about how, the day before Annie and I had taken Mum to the nursing home in Orono, I had gone up with her good patchwork quilt and feather pillows, her rocking chair with the tan corduroy cushion, some houseplants and her watering can. I put labels on the backs of the photos and placed them around her room. I tacked lace runners on the walls in swags and pinned Virgin Mary and Sacred Heart medals on them. I hung up her favorite picture of the Christ Child and a crucifix. I put her large-print Readers Digest books on the nightstand next to her clock with the lighted face. Then came the day. Annie and I picked Mum up at the hospital, and drove her to Orono. As we approached the nursing home, she said from the backseat, "Where are we, girls?"

We were quiet for a minute, thinking; then Annie said, "We are going to the nursing home in Orono that we talked about because Dr. Brown said you now require nursing care."

"Oh, I see," she said and continued to look out the windows, commenting about the big, white frame houses along the Bennock Road. Annie drove a bit slower, leaning forward to check on Mum in her rear-view mirror.

In a matter of minutes we pulled into the driveway at the nursing home. The long, gray, one-story clapboard building with white trim was quite new. Shrubs and bushes stepped out from the building in welcome. Columns flanked the institutional double glass doors. We pulled into a parking space next to them, and I helped Mum out. The chickadees announced their presence from the thick bushes. Mum called back, "Chick-a-dee-dee-dee!" Annie carried Mum's small green suitcase from the hospital. I pulled the door open. We stepped into a reception area. Couches and wing-backed chairs were grouped together around low wooden tables. The room was papered in a small floral pattern and was flooded in afternoon sunlight. No one was sitting there. A nattily dressed couple was speaking with the receptionist seated behind a curved oak desk connecting two parlor-like rooms. The man had dark curly hair, small close-set, dark eyes and he looked uncomfortable in his dark, three-piece suit. She was taller and younger with blond hair that tumbled over her pinstriped suit jacket. They looked like bankers. They turned as we entered and walked toward us. "Welcome, Mrs. LaFlamme," said the man, extending his hand to Mum, a gold bracelet tumbling out of his jacket sleeve.

"We hope you will be very comfortable and happy here with us," said the woman, smiling at Mum. The man stepped back to his wife's side, clasping his hands behind him, blinking his tiny, dark eyes.

Mother said, "Why, thank you." Then she cupped her hand and whispered to me, "Who are they?"

"They are the owners," I said. We all smiled politely at each other.

"Your room is the first one on the right," said the woman, turning her head, her golden hair cascading over her shoulders.

We walked slowly to the doorway, and the three of us stepped in. Mum's blue ginger-jar lamp was glowing, the one with the pleated white shade, and the late afternoon sun shone through the white, criss-cross ruffled curtains. Mum stepped up to the bed, touching her patchwork quilt. "Oh, my! Is this my room?" and she hurried to look at the little shrines on the walls.

"Yes, Mum," I said, turning so she could not see my sad face.

"Oh, Jo. This is the most beautiful room I've ever seen! Did you arrange everything like this?"

"Yes, I did."

She picked up one of the pictures of her great grandchildren. "Who is this beautiful child?" she asked.

"Turn it over, Mum." And I showed her the label that said, Meaghan, Tess's granddaughter, age 2. She was utterly delighted as she read one after another. I did not bring a picture of Daddy. We no longer mentioned him because she suffered anew each time.

She had told Annie one time, "I can't find Daddy. I took a cab and went downtown, but his barber shop isn't there." She began to cry. "He didn't come home all night."

Annie had sat her down and held her hands and said, "Mum, Daddy is dead."

"Oh! My God!" she screamed, bursting into tears, falling into a chair grief-stricken. "When, darlin', when?"

"Last year, Mummy."

"Oh! My God in Heaven! Why didn't you tell me? I would have had a funeral! Oh, dear God, my poor Joe!" We could not console her. It happened several times. Sometimes she wept for days. Then one day she stopped asking about him. Her husband of over fifty years had slipped down the stairs of her mind.

Now, with memories lingering like ghosts, I saw the lights of Bangor in the distance. I would be at Annie's soon. This was my thirty-sixth trip in eighteen months. I could sense more and more how fragile are the threads that connect Mum to the present, and how strong the cords that tether her to the past.

The next day was cold and dazzling, with the sun tossing diamonds off the snow. The evening before, Annie and I had avoided the topic of Mum. Now, driving to Orono, I broached it. "How do you think Mum is this week?"

"I haven't been up. I can't go every day now. I can't endure it. I miss her so much; and then I come here and I'm a wreck for days." Annie recently had stopped biting her fingernails by gluing on fake ones. Today they were painted a dusty rose. She began to drive, holding the steering wheel with her thumbs and extending her fingers, lacquer-side up, like fans.

"Perhaps every day is just too much..."

"You have never been here every day like I've been. Mum and I have been together every day of my life. I love her so much. I thought when Dad died so suddenly, I could make it up to her, take her places, but that's not what happened. How can you stand this?"

"For the last year or so I've pretended she is a new mother, one God sent as the transitional mother. I just go to where her woolly mind is and play with her."

"At least she knows your name! Most of the time she thinks I am Tess." She reached into her purse between us, never taking her eyes off the road. "Mint?" she asked and shook two little green candies into her lap.

"No, thanks," I said. "Don't you think that your physical changes add to this confusion? You've lost so much weight, dear, that even the relatives ask if it's you."

"Sometimes I wonder how long this can go on." Click. Click. Click. She snapped her new thumbnail against the index nail. "How long can you keep up your pretense of cheerfulness?"

The car seemed crowded as if sadness and gloom had filled up the backseat. I took in a deep breath. "It often doesn't hit me until a day later. Then I cry and rail at God about this cruel trick. Sometimes I think I am already in mourning and that when she dies, I won't be one bit sadder." I shivered and stared straight ahead.

"I did call the doctor this past week, and he says she is on a plateau, that her condition could remain stable. Oh, how I hate that word could!"

"I thank the heavens she is here in Orono. Gosh, remember how horrified we all were when Dr. Brown said 'nursing home'?" The car's heater sent out a gust of warm air.

"It didn't help that the only ones we had ever been in were death traps," Annie said, her voice rising with the accelerator.

"Do you want me to drive?" I asked.

"No. I'm just fine."

I was staring out the side window. A family of snowmen seemed to dash by. "How did you know about this place?"

"Don't you dare get forgetful! The owners are clients where I work! Remember?" She raked her fingers through her short, curly brown hair. "Mostly this nursing home has people like Mum, although there is that one wing with the tragically bedridden. But even that has a cheerfulness somehow, and it doesn't reek of urine like where poor Aunt Mary clung to life." The air from the heater dislodged a little puff of cigarette smoke from some hidden crack, reminding me that we used to drive along laughing, smoking like chimneys, the radio blaring.

After a brief silence I said, "Sometimes I think I can't smile through the dining room routine one more time. I watch Mum hurry to find her place card, then exclaim when she finds it where it always is, and shyly introduce herself to the same women. Then they all introduce themselves to her, too, none of them recalling their previous meals together."

Click. Click. Click. This time it was the directional signal. Annie's voice slowed with the car. "Well, if she can't keep her daughters straight in her mind..."

Then we were there, at the nursing home. It was just past noon. The tires crunched over the hard-packed snow as we pulled into the parking area.

As we entered, Stella the receptionist's dark blond head popped up, calling hello. Stella loved red. Today she had on a red paisley blouse with ruffles on the collar and cuffs. Her nursing home name badge was lost in the profusion.

"Hello, Stella," I said. "How is Mum doing?"

"As she says, 'nary an ache!' You know, she's teaching me about the birds. I saw a bunch of them around the feeders last week, and I asked her to come out and tell me what they were. She said they were young grackles, and even though they looked beautiful with their iridescent green and blue caps, they were not pleasant birds, and that few blackbirds are!" Stella's full lips, painted a vivid red, curved up in a smile revealing a little fleck of lipstick on one of her front teeth. "Then she hurried to her room to get her bird book so I could see what they looked like in silhouette — the way we see them when they fly,' she said." Stella paused for air.

Annie, shifting her shoulder bag, looked like a young version of Mum today. "No more problems with her running away like she did last Thursday?"

"No, thank heavens! She gave us quite a scare when she headed down the road like that. Luckily, a neighbor saw her and brought her back in the car. We still don't think she needs an alarm bracelet because she has always gone out on the grounds to feed the birds."

Our parents' love of birds was always selective. After Dad's retirement, he set a regime in place. The feeders were filled the very first thing in the morning with thistle seeds, except for the feeder in the back of the yard, hooked to the stockade fence. This had a mixture of seeds. "It's for the bigger birds. It also keeps 'em away from the songbirds," Dad had said. When the fruit tree in the far corner of the garden had to be cut down, Dad nailed a trash-can cover upside down on the trunk. Then he placed the big statue of St. Francis on it and filled the lid with the seed mixture. "It's for the squirrels," he said. "It keeps them away from the songbirds' food." All the songbird feeders were hung from the apple tree just beyond the kitchen window. Below it was a cement birdbath, one of the few things in the yard he did not paint aluminum or turquoise.

Dad kept a little pile of stones on the redwood-stained picnic table, handy to throw at unwelcome birds or neighborhood cats who dared venture into his sanctuary.

There was a small tool shed just to the left of the apple tree where he stored paint, birdseed, and his mother's good dishes until the day he found mouse droppings on the carton and a torn bag of seed. He stopped right then that early morning and broke each dish with a hammer. "He had no choice," said Mummy, weeping when I phoned her that night. "The mice had walked all over them."

His was not a peaceful retirement, holding back the onslaught of nature in his own backyard. For the first year after his death, Mum maintained the yard regime; but soon all sorts of birds flew in to eat, squirrels hung upside down off the songbird feeders, even pigeons roamed freely, eating seeds that had fallen to the ground. They all flapped off when Bill Bishop's cat climbed over the fence. "They're all God's creatures, and I love every one of them," Mum had said.

Now Stella leaned forward and took a sip from a tan plastic coffee mug. Her eyes lost their sparkle and she said, "Y'know, when we asked your mother why she ran down the road, she said she was looking for her mother." Stella shook her head, her short curls bouncing in the aftershock. "It's heartbreaking!" Then she reached for the phone, waving us forward with the other hand. "Go ahead. She's been watching for you."

Mum must have heard our voices, for she stepped out into the hall. "Jo, when did you get here?"

"Just now, sweetheart," I said. "How do you feel today?"

"Nary an ache nor pain," she said, rushing to hug us.

"Great! We're here to do the fall cleaning," I said. Annie and I entered her room, close behind her. Annie went right away to the closet and began organizing it. As a teenager, Annie and our Mother had whole days when they would not speak to each other. When Annie was fifteen, she was the only daughter left at home. She was torn between feeling abandoned by her sisters and wishing Mum would leave so she could live alone with Dad. Sometimes, seemingly for no reason, she would run to her room, slam the door, and refuse to come out for hours. Or she would eat an entire meal, speaking only with Dad, as if Mum was not there. Then after Annie's daughter was born, everything changed between them. They became inseparable until this brain disease walled them off again. Today I sensed Annie's silence was filled with longing. She methodically took out all the shoes, separating them from balled-up panty hose, the empty hangers clinking above her head like cymbals.

I began with the dresser drawers. Throughout her lifetime, the contents of Mum's bureaus were always arranged in neat little rows. Now they were a tangle of clothes, underwear and ribbon candy — this metaphor of her mind.

Holding up a fistful of panties, I said, "Good news, Mummy. You won't be bare-ass anymore. Look! Lots of them."

"Oh, they're not mine, dear. I don't know whose they are."

"Yes, look here, sweetheart. Your name is right on them."

She stared at them as if this wasn't her name and said, "Oh, I didn't know."

"That's OK," I said, picking some broken ribbon candy off another pair. "Wait a minute," I teased, "these panties say Sawyer. Eileen, are you stealing panties? Are you in on panty raids living this near the University?"

"Merciful God, no!" Then she stared at the name. "Sawyer? I

don't know who that is."

"Quick," I said to Mother, "go toss 'em down the laundry chute before someone calls the cops."

She loved the joke of it and grabbed the large blue panties and dashed across the hall and dropped them down the chute. She looked both ways, as if crossing a road, before dashing back into the room.

"Well," she said, hurrying toward me, "where are you going to sleep tonight?"

"At Annie's."

Then she turned and looked at Annie with her bright blue eyes and said, "And you, dear. Where are you going to sleep?"

"Mother, I am Annie." Annie turned away and chewed on the edge of one of her dusty-rose fingernails before putting a stack of folded sweaters on the shelf. It pained them both, but there wasn't even a flicker of recognition in Mum's eyes. She could not place this woman, her youngest daughter, with whom she had shared her daily life for over forty years.

Mum turned to me and asked in a stage whisper, "Is it really Annie?"

"Yes, Mum, it is."

"Why don't I remember?" Her hands grasped either side of her face.

"Because you have a brain disease. It must be very scary for you. Are you scared?"

"Oh, yes, darlin'. Sometimes I don't know if I even had lunch. Or where I was before I was here. Yet, I can remember Mae and me working in Hogan's Bakery when we were just teenagers. We would get up at 4 AM. Walk there in the dark. It wasn't far, just up at the top of Parker Street, and Mama said, 'just follow your nose' because the smell of bread baking floated down from the top of that hill! We'd put on our white aprons (we had to fold them over because we were just little girls), and then we'd do our job of flipping the big loaves out of the pans and spreading butter on the rounded tops. We each earned twenty cents a week, and we got one loaf of bread a day. I can remember how happy we were, my sister and me." She was ebullient now, eyes glistening.

"Well, you remember the way-back past, and I'll do this week. OK?" She nodded and stole another glance at Annie, who was arranging clothes by size: blouses first, then skirts, then dresses. I said, "Now, let's see, Mum. You've got twelve pairs of panties, six bras, a half slip — and oh — I stopped by the house and got you twelve pairs of panty hose!" I took them out of my handbag and passed them to her.

She began adding one more neat row to the drawer. Then she looked up into my face, came close and whispered, "Did Mama send you?" Her mother had been dead for thirty years.

"Why, yes, she did, Mum."

"Oh, I'm so glad. I've been calling her old number and nothing happens. Then I called information, but they don't have a listing. Not even one for Leo. I think Mama's is disconnected. Maybe she hasn't enough money." She was right on the verge of tears.

"I'll check, darlin', and I'll take care of it."

"Oh, thank you, honey. I don't know why she hasn't come by. I can't find Mae or Dan either." These brothers and sisters were all dead. Annie had letters returned to her that Mum had written to them, asking them to come visit.

"I'll get in touch with them for you. Do you want me to tell them that you are feeling pretty good?"

She was visibly relieved. "Tell them, nary an ache nor pain!"

"I will, darlin'. Now let's go get some coffee and cake."

"First, will you fix my hair? I love the way you do it." I pulled open the nightstand, took out her hairbrush, and fluffed up the snow-white curls. I reached in for the rose lipstick, drew a line on her cupid-bow lips, and daubed a dot on either cheek, blending it toward her cheekbones. All the while she stared at me, bright-blue eyes twinkling. Then she dashed for the mirror in the bathroom and exclaimed, "Glory be to God, for this is none of I!" This little phrase had not tumbled down the stairs of her mind. It was one she had used all our lives when fate delighted her. She dashed back, carrying the pair of laundered panties from the towel bar and tucked them into her purse.

We went shopping for a new lipstick, took a drive along the river while Mum told us in vivid detail about how her Aunt Mamie worked on Indian Island in the parish house. Then we stopped at Mum's favorite place on the Bennock Road for dessert. We got our cake and coffee and talked about anything that popped into our heads, like how long cream lasts in those tiny white containers and how birds know the exact dates to migrate.

"Now some birds never go far from home," Mum said, gesturing with her pinkie while holding her fork. "Those little wrens don't go much farther than down to the corner and back, but they are just as precious to God as the elegant grosbeaks that swoop down on their way through in April." The little wrens were strung on a wire across from the restaurant, brown beads in a necklace. Mum took a bite of cake laden with chocolate frosting and continued, "I've already fed that bunch today."

I asked, "Is it true that birds who frequent bird feeders decide not to migrate?"

Mum's quick laugh escaped like a sneeze. "Heavens, no, sweetheart! You couldn't keep a migrating bird here if you tried. The wrens are like me. They stick close to home. The feeders keep them alive."

Annie pushed her empty plate to one side and said, "Be careful when you go out to fill the feeders, Mum. It's quite icy right now."

"Oh, don't worry, darlin'. Dad shovels for me every day."

This was the first time she had mentioned Dad in such a long time. Annie and I exchanged heightened glances. Annie said, "Dad does?"

She looked up quickly, first at me, then Annie, and smiled her quizzical little smile. "Oh, not your dad, dear, my dad. He's out there first thing in the mornin'."

Mum seemed to be tired now or engrossed in the cake eating. She pressed each remaining chocolate crumb between the tines of the stainless steel fork and then lapped them off. She caught the one remaining morsel with her index finger and popped it into her mouth. "Scrumptious," she said. It was time to head back. Annie went to the front to pay the check while I helped Mum get into her coat.

We walked outside in the windy afternoon. "Mum," I said, "did you know you have a button missing from your blouse?"

"Yes, it popped off this morning when I was getting dressed. I would have sewed it back on, but I don't have a needle and thread," she said as we walked toward the car. Annie told Mum she saw her sewing basket when she was working in the closet and that we would get it out for her when we got back to the nursing home.

We piled into the car, and Annie began coaxing the heater to warm up. As she pulled out on the road, Mum lost her balance and tipped over on the backseat, her seat belt holding her fast. I was unbuckled in a flash, leaned over and sat her back up. She looked perplexed, so I said, "Eileen, have you been drinking again?"

"Saints preserve us!" she laughed. "You are so wicked today." And to Annie she said, "Isn't she wicked, er..." and clearly she had again forgotten her name. She had always referred to Annie as "a gift from God when we least expected it." Now, she leaned forward a bit to look at her, searching for a connection.

When we came into the lobby area of the nursing home, two of the residents sitting in the reception/parlor smiled and said hello. Mother said to us, "Did you know Cousin Betty lives here?" Her cousin had been dead for twenty years. Mum walked over to a tall woman and said, "Two of my girls are here today, Betty. Isn't that nice?"

The woman, dressed in a lilac-colored crepe dress, seemed pleased. She stood up and walked gingerly toward us, her feet in long, narrow purple suede pumps. She extended her gloved hand and said formally to both of us, "How do you do." Mum's round face was glowing pink as Annie and I shook the woman's hand.

Stella came from behind the desk. "Hi, Eileen. Tell me what you did with your daughters." She wore a fragrance that hung heavy on the air compared to Mum's Lily of the Valley.

"Oh, lots of things, didn't we?"

"We had triple chocolate cake..."

"Scrumptious," interrupted Mum.

"Oh, Eileen," said Stella, "I think I heard a robin this afternoon!"

Mum said, "Did it sound like this?" Then she whistled the lyrical little tut tut tut trill the way she used to when she hung the washing out on the lines. Sometimes a robin called back, and we could never tell them apart.

"Why, Eileen, you'll have robins walking right in the front door," said Stella in utter amazement.

Mum smiled and took Stella to one side and said, "The robin has several songs, all very distinctive, but once you know them, you can tell a robin, sight unseen." Annie and I had smug little smiles on our faces. Our mother was present, right here. Then Mum said, "Stella, do you know how the robin got its red breast?"

Stella grasped one of Mum's hands. "Why no, Eileen. You tell me."

"A robin, beneath the cross at Calvary, carried the Blessed Mother's tears in its beak to quench Jesus' thirst. Just as it was giving a drop to drink, blood came down Jesus' forehead from the crown of thorns and the dear robin blotted it away from Jesus' eyes with its chest. Every robin born since the time of Jesus has had a red breast." Mum finished, pursed her cupid-bow lips and folded her arms in schoolgirl fashion. "That's why we call 'em robin redbreast. It's a very old bird," she said, her voice trailing off to a whisper.

Stella's eyes were wide. "Why, Eileen, is that in your bird book?"

"Oh, no dear. My mother told me when I was just a little girl." Then Mum walked, arms still folded, toward her room. Annie and I followed her in. I opened her closet and got her sewing kit. "Is that mine, darlin'?" she asked.

"Yes, Mum. I brought it here some time ago. Remember this little pin cushion Mia got you in San Francisco's Chinatown?" Mia had been up from Portland last week to take Mum out and had met the new Cousin Betty then. "And your favorite scissors?" Mum smiled that quizzical little smile, not remembering these things. I said, "Let me thread the needle for you, darlin'."

Annie passed her a blouse. "Why don't you change into this, Mum?" And our Mother, a paragon of modesty, just took her blouse off, not noticing that we were there or that her door was open.

I picked up the sweaters and pulled the rocker next to her bed, spreading out her white blouse. "Do you have the button, Mum?"

"Oh, yes, darlin'." She reached into the pocket of her red, double-knit slacks and pulled out the button, holding it up the way we did when we played, "Button, Button, Who's Got the Button!" She was all smiles. Then it was time to go.

"We'll be back in the morning, Mum," I said, bending down to kiss her. "We love you." Annie kissed her, too.

We stepped outside; a flock of purple finches swooped past us. There seemed to be dozens of them. Their caps and tail feathers shown scarlet in the low afternoon sun. The air was filled with their fast, melodic songs as they vied for the perches on the feeders that swung from the red oak that still clung fast to its leaves.

We walked toward the car. I could see into Mum's room through the white, criss-cross ruffled curtains. She sat with her back toward us in the glow of the lamplight, completely absorbed in the task of sewing as if she were home at the kitchen table. She moistened her index finger and rolled the white thread between it and her thumb. She made a knot. She began slowly to sew.

I heard a phone ring far away and opened my eyes. The little red lights on the guestroom clock read 5:15. I heard my sister speaking quietly.

"Hello…Yes, this is she…What is that?…When did it happen?" She spoke a bit more but I could not hear her. Then I saw her standing in the doorway.

"What's wrong"?

"That was the nursing home. Mum is dead. They found her a few minutes ago. She was completely dressed and had made her bed. Then she collapsed." Annie still spoke quietly, almost in a whisper.

"Do you think they had the right number?" I asked.

"Yes, Jo, Mum is gone. Let's go downstairs and decide what time to call our sisters." She bent over under the weight of her own sad words.

I got up and followed her slowly down the stairs, the dark house now devoid of air. Mum's four sweaters were on towels on the radiators in the front hall. I touched them. They were not yet dry.

Chowdah
- *1990* -

It's a warm spring morning, and I'm in my loft at the computer when the phone rings. "Hello, darlin'. Are you busy?" It's Marian.

"I plan to work on my writing all day, dear. I'm doing a brochure for the medical center. What do you need?"

"Will you come over sometime today and peel two potatoes for me?"

"Sure, Marian. It would be best if I came right now."

"I'm not interfering with your writing, am I? I mean, if you feel inspired you could come later."

"No, it's best if I come right now."

I drive to Marian's, picking up two Cokes on the way. I often wonder if Marian sits across town, dreaming up things for me to do for her.

I pull in to the parking lot in front of the high-rise and take the elevator to the seventh floor. As I start down the long, narrow hall, I can see her standing in the open doorway of her apartment. With the light behind her, she looks as though she's cut from black construction paper.

"Hi, darlin'," she calls out in her raspy voice.

"Hi, Marian."

"HAHAHA! It must be spring. You've got shorts on."

"Yes, thank heavens!" I say, opening the paper bag I brought. "I got us Cokes."

"I've already got some. My homemaker was here on Thursday. Come in. I know you're gonna say it smells like the Elks Lodge in here. You are, aren't you?"

The cigarette smoke would have floored a herd of four-legged elk. I gasp, taking shallow breaths as I head across the room to the window. I pull open the slider and see that the big maple trees adjacent to the high-rise are about to bud.

"I wanted to spray before you got here. You do it, darlin'."

There is a can of air freshener on the green kitchen counter near the sink. I grab it and spray the rug, chair and drapes. "This smells like ribbon candy."

"HAHAHA!" laughs Marian. She is standing in the middle of the room, striped with a gentle light from the Venetian blinds.

I want to make this visit brief. "Marian, where are the potatoes?"

"Right there on the kitchen counter," she says. Then her head drops down until she is nearly looking at her knees. She backs up and flops down on the couch, still folded over. "Once you peel 'em I'll come show you how I want 'em cut. They're for fish chowdah." She begins to cough and wheeze. "I just need a little help today."

I peel the potatoes as fast as I can. "Diced or chunks?" I ask.

She gets up and staggers into the kitchen, an alcove off her living room.

"I'll show you," she gasps, taking the knife from me and attempting to push it into the potato.

"Marian, let me cut it; then you show me what size," I say, trying to get the knife out of her wobbly hand. "Have you lost more weight?"

"Yes," she wheezes. "Like this," she says, whacking through the potato. "Now I weigh 90 pounds."

"Sit down, Marian. I can do this." I help her back to the couch. There are little stuffed animals lined up along the back — some with missing eyes, all with a dusty, forlorn appearance. Marian told me once that a woman in the building collects them from the Salvation Army and delivers them from floor to floor. Marian has about twenty now.

"Did you get a Mother's Day card from your son?" she asks.

"No, dear," I say matter-of-factly, walking back to the kitchen.

"I didn't get any from my boys neither, Jo." Her mouth begins to open and close like a baby bird's. "I know you are busy and have your own advertising company and all. I'll bet you don't even remember when we first met, when you came to visit your parents across the street. I made you coffee and cookies more than once. You probably can't remember that, can you?" She is rocking back and forth on the couch with her arms tightly folded, grasping her sides.

"Yes, I do, Marian."

She stifles a cough. "Do you remember our little boys?"

"I sure do. Let's see. Scott must be forty; Gary, thirty-five because my son's thirty-six now. Time has flown..."

"Now put the potatoes in a pan and just barely cover them with water."

I do as instructed.

"Now turn the burner on high until it comes to a boil. Not that burner! The one on the right." The baby bird becomes a hawk, voice soaring.

"Marian, where are the onions?" I know now that I have really been summoned to make fish chowder.

"I got the frozen ones. Get 'em out, but don't add 'em yet. Tell me when the potatoes are boiling."

"Is William coming for chowder?" I ask.

"Maybe. Maybe not. I had to hang up on him last night. Jo, it's a terrible problem. William can't do anything right. I asked him to pick up Memorial Day flowers, and he got all wound up, saying I'd only criticize him if he didn't get the ones I wanted. How hard can that be!" she says, her eyes open wide — unblinking, protruding.

"Did he get them?" I ask.

"Yes, of course, but not until I got really angry at him about pink geraniums."

"Marian, William has been a darn good friend to you all these years."

"He has no patience," she hollers. "You know what he said to me when he took me out riding? He got on a one-way street, and I yelled at him to make a U-turn. And he said —are you listening? — he said, 'I could kill you, Marian!' See what I have been putting up with all these years?"

"When did that happen, Marian?"

"Last year."

"Chances are he didn't plan to kill you, dear. It's just an expression."

"Well, thank God, I never married him. Is the water boiling?"

"Yes."

"Add the onions…half that bag. Let me see first how many you're adding."

I pour half the bag into a dish and walk over to the couch to show her. "Add some more," she says and then begins rocking again.

"Marian, would you like me to cut up the fish?"

"Not yet. Wait until the onions are cooked."

She gets up and sidesteps as if she is on a listing ship, then patters off in the opposite direction right into the kitchen next to where I am standing. I ask, "How can I help, Marian?"

She lifts the lid and looks into the pot. "Too much water," she says. "Get the fish out of the fridge. It's on the bottom shelf."

I get the fish and unwrap it. It is a stunning piece of haddock.

"Now wash it and don't get it near the blue sponge. That's for dishes." She tosses the sponge behind the faucets. "Put it here. I'll show you. I want big chunks, like this." She gives the fish three whacks with the big knife, leaving creases for me to follow. "Put it in, skin side down."

"Marian, it's skinless."

"I know that! Put it in with the outside of the fish down so that it won't break apart."

I cut the three pieces and slip them into the steaming kettle.

"Now turn down the boil immediately and add the milk." She ricochets back to the couch.

"Would you like me to get you some, Marian?"

"No, just leave it. Did you add butter?"

"No, but I can," I say, returning to the refrigerator one more time. I notice she has six bottles of Coke.

"Why don't you have a bowl? It smells bee-U-tee-ful!" Marian exclaims. "What's your hurry?"

It is one-thirty in the afternoon. "I need to get back. I'll set your bowl, spoon and crackers out and reduce the heat to simmer."

"Thanks, darlin'. My social worker says, 'When you need help, Marian, ask.' So I do. Don't you ever need help?" But before I can answer she yells, "Take that stinkin' fish wrapper with you."

"I've got it right here with the trash from the kitchen. Let me have your ashtray." There must be twenty red-rimmed butts crammed in it.

Marian passes it to me and says, "Don't make that face. You used to smoke." She grabs her inhaler. "The oxygen isn't much use. This helps a little (swoosh) but my doctor says my real problem is stress, and nothing seems to help that. What do you do for stress, darlin'?" Her eyes are brimming.

"I make soup."

She erupts with laughter. "My God, you're a riot! HAHAHA. Now give me a big hug, darlin'. And don't be such a stranger."

Single White Male
– 1993 –

The three of us have been meeting for breakfast at the Miss Portland Diner every Friday for over a year. There is my younger sister, Mia, a real-estate broker who moved to Portland with her husband in the late '80s. The real-estate boom was over here, but Mia had been selling in our hometown of Bangor for ten years and was not at all discouraged by the market. In fact, Mia is rarely discouraged. She makes a calm presentation of herself, but I know she is a lot like the ducks we see on our walks — calm on top of the water, feet paddling furiously below. She dresses like the successful broker that she is, wearing tailored but vibrantly colored two-piece dresses and suits splashed with jewelry and her gold multi-million–dollar producer pin. Even her gym clothes are coordinated, matching the green and purple trim in her Reebok cross trainers.

We were a breakfast duo until Phil joined us. Phil has close-cropped white hair, remarkably long arms and medium height and build. He always wears a gray sweat suit. If the day is warm he peels off a layer and has a short, lighter-weight version underneath. Phil is in his early 70s, a retired executive who still consults from time to time. Sometimes I imagine Phil flying around the country, carrying his briefcase, still dressed in his gray sweats. We first noticed him at our Lifeline class at the University. He was a fixture each Monday, Wednesday and Friday. One week he didn't show up. I asked the instructor about him, and she said his wife had died. I bought a card, signed my name and Mia's, and mailed it off that very day. A week later he was back. During the cool-down exercises Phil thanked us for the card. He looked so very sad that I invited him to join us for breakfast. We have been a threesome ever since.

As for me, I am about the same size as my sister, although at 5'3"
she is quick to remind me she is a full inch taller and eighteen months
younger. My gym attire differs only slightly from Phil's. I have a dark-
blue, long-sleeved, long pants set and a light-blue, short-sleeved, short
pants set. However, I only wear one outfit at a time with a windbreaker.

I have not dated since my divorce — that was twenty-six years
ago! Initially I regarded men as dangerous, then burdensome. Then I
just sort of forgot about them. But I do have lots of men friends. They
are either married or gay. I noticed in a magazine article that these
are called safe men. One of my favorite of these safe men is Hilton,
who was married when I met him nineteen years ago — a fact he kept
from me for several months. He has long been on his own. When I
tell friends how I met him, it sounds so bizarre, but it really wasn't!
I was coming back to my loft after dinner one summer night, and I
saw a gentleman with his hands cupped against the window pane, his
head pressed against them, peering into my entrance door. He didn't
look like a Peeping Tom, more like a professor who had misplaced
something. I remember stepping up behind him and saying, "What
are you looking at?" He jumped back, pulled a navy bandanna from his
crumpled cotton jacket, mopped his brow, and said, "Forgive me. Do
you live here? I've been fascinated by the amount of hammering so I
thought...Hello, I'm Hilton McGuire." He extended his right hand and
shoved the bandanna back in his pocket with the other. "I live next
door on the third floor."

I invited him up to see the loft, already a topic of conversation
in town as it was a third-story barn that had been converted to a
spectacular apartment. "My walls back up to this one," said Hilton,
"and I knew from the level of hammering that crew must be hard at
it. Then the pounding stopped last week, and I've been curious ever
since." There was that word "been," sounding like bean. I asked him if
he was British, and he was quick to say that he had bean born in New
Zealand. After that tour of my apartment, we would often see each
other on the street. Then we began going to films at the college and
sometimes cooking supper for each other. The first night he invited
me to his apartment for dinner, he proudly set a loaf of some sort on

the table. He placed a cold slice of it on my plate. I sat there looking at it, trying to decide what it was. There were chunks of meat held together with a clear gelatin. "Trotters in Aspic," he said with a sigh of achievement.

I tasted it gingerly. It reminded me of a coarse, country paté. I nibbled at it again. "Tell me, Hilton, how did you make this?" That's when I discovered I was eating pigs feet in Jell-O!

Just recently, I was remembering the time I made a blender full of lethal rum drinks and then crawled from my balcony overlooking the river across two loose planks to Hilton's fire escape. I knocked on his window, and he was genuinely startled to see someone outside his third-story apartment. He had on a navy wool bathrobe, open, revealing a white undershirt and boxer shorts.

"Hey, Hilton," I said, clinging tightly to the boards, "wanna come over for cocktails?"

"Why, yes. That would be lovely, but first I'll need to dress."

"No, you don't. Just crawl across the boards to my balcony."

He did, and we had a great time talking about books and telling each other stories. When the drinks were gone, he said he felt a bit tipsy. "Oh, dear, I shan't be able to go home the way I came." That meant going from my front door across the sidewalk to his entrance in the heart of downtown Auburn.

"Let's go," I said. "I'll be the lookout." Down the two flights of stairs we went. I stepped outside and, when there was no one walking by, I whispered, "The coast is clear!" Hilton dashed out, clutching his bathrobe, barelegged, and made a mad dash for his door, but not before the diners in the window seats at the little cafe between our buildings looked up at him. He called later to say that it had all bean very exciting.

That's what I mean by safe. I had spent the entire evening with a man in his bathrobe and underwear, and he was perfectly mannered.

So on one of our walks, when I tell Mia I'm thinking about finding a sweetheart, she is amazed. I tell her I'm thinking about speaking to Hilton about my feelings for him. She reminds me he already has a sweetheart. I remind her Hilton has had women friends before; yet we continue to talk every week, exchange books, and eat together. "Now he did move in with this last woman but has since moved out. He was looking at condos in Portland just last month."

"Give him my card," Mia says, then flies into action, pointing out men at the gym and asking if I want to be introduced to a certain someone at the yacht club. I begin to regret revealing my fledgling thoughts to her.

Now it is Friday at the Miss Portland Diner and Mia has brought me a voice introduction personals page from the Maine Sunday Telegram.

"Read this," she says, unzipping her mint-green windbreaker, tossing it ahead of her into the wine leatherette booth. "This guy sounds perfect for you, and it's time you stopped merely thinking about men and met somebody. You don't want to end up like Marian, do you?" Marian is about five years older than I am. We met her when she lived across the street from our parents back thirty years ago. She has emphysema, chain-smokes, takes medication for depression and chases it with alcohol. Mia's reference is not about Marian's health. It's about Marian's desperate loneliness.

I slide into the booth beside Mia. Phil sits down across from us, asking, "What's this?" He picks up the folded newspaper.

Mia pulls off her mint-green headband, fluffs up her red hair and says, "Gimme that." Then she reads it, a bit louder than I think is necessary. "Writer, SWM, late 50s, seeks NS/SWW who enjoys romantic walks on the beach, theater and slow dancing. H/W proportionate. See? He's perfect. Call him."

The waitress, wearing a Miss Portland Diner T-shirt and a short, black skirt, walks up to our booth and says, "The usual?" Her blond, fuzzy hair is trapped under a coarse, black hairnet. Instead of writing down our order, she taps the index finger of her right hand as if sending Morse code to the kitchen. "Two teas, milk, one coffee. Three cups of oats, a pinch of brown sugar, one order of grilled biscuits and jelly? Right?"

"That's perfect," I say, picking up the newspaper.

"Don't forget the ice water," says Phil, whose turn it is to pay. He grasps the right sleeve of his sweatshirt with his left hand and pulls it down over his right hand. Then holding the cuff with his fingers, he draws his arm back and forth like some gigantic windshield wiper until he is satisfied that his place at the table is clean.

"Mia, what do all these letters mean? SWM and NS?" I ask.

Mia leans forward and in a near whisper says, "SWM means single white male and NS means non-smoking." She is clearly delighted with herself.

It is warm in here today and I pull off my windbreaker. "Mia, how do you know these things?" I ask in amazement.

"It's across the bottom of the page," she says glibly, pointing at it with her diamond-laden finger.

Phil takes off his glasses, where a smudge is always lurking, and rubs at them with a tiny napkin from the chrome dispenser on the end of our table. He says, "You know, Mother always used to say..." Then he looks up as the waitress brings the tumblers of ice water, the teas and coffee. He dips the corner of the napkin in his glass and rubs the hated smudge off one lens.

I say, "I don't think I'd dare call up someone I don't even know."

Mia pulls the string of her tea bag up and down as if it were a yo-yo. "That's the whole point. You don't know any men. Remember how Annie found Bob through the personals? She called him up, they got together and BINGO! It's how people meet today. When they were in town a week ago they seemed real happy. You know you could learn a thing or two from our baby sister." She lifts the tea bag out of the cup and places it on her saucer. Then she holds up the little octagonal card attached by string to the tea bag. "Mine says, 'Always forgive your enemies. Seldom does anything annoy them more.' That's brilliant," she says. Phil's smile reveals bicuspids with gold fillings.

"What does yours say?" Phil asks me.

I had read it moments earlier. "It says, 'A penny saved is only a penny.' Perhaps I could get work at the tea bag factory, writing little phrases."

Mia returns to the topic. "Give this guy a call."

"I don't think I want to leave my name and number for just anyone to call me."

Mia is ready. "If he doesn't sound interesting, just hang up."

Phil, who often assures us he has inherited his mother's sense of thrift, says, "A penny saved is a penny earned. Mother, God rest her soul, knew just exactly how to collect pennies one at a time. Ben Franklin had her in mind when he wrote that." Phil took a sip of his ice water. "Father used to say, 'A penny pinched has been in Mother's grasp.' Oh, she was thrifty. Perhaps a little tight when it came to gift giving." Phil sighs. "You know," he says, gazing into his glass, "she left me quite a nest egg. No one was more surprised than I at what she had amassed." Then to remind us it is his turn to pay, he places a ten-dollar bill on the table near the napkin holder. "Now, Mia, is there a charge to put an ad in the paper?" he asks.

Mia lowers her teacup. "No, the caller pays $2.19 per minute. It's a 900 number."

The waitress brings the oatmeal and biscuits. We eat while talking about our weekend plans. Phil is building storage drawers into the eaves in his attic. "I went down to Rufus-Deering Lumber and they have the whole outfit in a kit. There are the drawers and the frame," he says while sprinkling brown sugar on his oatmeal. He always waits to be last for the brown sugar, which assures him of the most generous portion.

"I'm painting my hall off-white," says Mia. Then she pushes the remaining half-biscuit toward me, for it is my job to cut it in equal thirds. Before Phil came, we'd each have a whole biscuit. A hush falls while I cut it.

"Perfect!" says Phil. "And you, Jo? What are you planning to do this weekend?"

"No grandchildren this weekend, so I am planning to write. Perhaps I'll have a pizza delivered late Saturday afternoon, and I have a new book. So, I'll have a wonderful time," I say.

"Be sure to call this guy," says Mia, scraping the last bit of jelly out of the tiny plastic container. Then she pushes the ad forward with her pinkie finger encircled by a tiny ring of garnets.

For the next week, whenever the topic of personal ads comes up, I tell Mia I haven't found the time to call, have even misplaced the paper. Then the following Sunday, the page resurfaces. I have spent the week working on a big writing project, a historical cookbook, and whatever came up during the week that did not relate to this project I tossed into my in-box, an old floral hatbox that was my mother's. Today, since it is a rainy day, I decide to sort out all the stuff and organize for the coming week. My office is in my home so I have the luxury of doing this task while still in my flannel nightie with a pot of tea handy to my computer. I begin by placing paper into related piles around my office: all unanswered phone calls on the velvet couch, faxes to be filed in job jackets there on the copy machine, unopened bills on the white rug, correspondence next to the cat, and so on. The next piece of paper is the personals page. I stare at it. Even if I want to call, I can't imagine how. Then I see it. There along the left-hand side of the page is a block of type, "To Listen & Respond." It outlines how to make a call. I read it twice. Then I dial the 900 number and enter the four-digit code for "Writer, SWM, late 50s."

A voice says, "Hi. Dis here's Boy-knee. I write tear-ter reviews for a weekly in southern Maine, so I gets to lotsa plays. I don't drink. I don't smoke. But, if yous do, that's OK. I'm a big guy, a six foota, NOT fat (chuckle, chuckle). I'm a salesman for a national siding company, NOT aluminum…vinyl. So if yous like ta git togetter, leaf ya name and numba. I ain't lookin fer no Venus DiMillo but if a woman's good lookin (chuckle, chuckle), so much da betta. So leaf a message and Boy-knee will call ya."

I hang up. I think of Hilton's voice with its soft New Zealand accent. I call Hilton and leave a message on his answering machine. I tell him about the big Queen Anne two-family house I saw for sale near the park and that maybe we could look at it, maybe buy it together. I ask him to call me.

Early the next morning Hilton calls. "Oh, Hilton," I say, reaching for my cup of tea, "when I saw the house I thought of how happy I was when you were my tenant in the big house in Lewiston. Didn't we have great times?"

"I think back with great affection on those years," Hilton says.

"Should I go look at it? Mia could show it to me. Maybe we could buy it together!"

"Why not, deah. Let me know the particulars," he says. Then we say good-bye.

The next Friday at the Miss Portland Diner we all arrive at about the same time. Phil hangs up his gray sweat shirt and I pull off my windbreaker. I announce before the oatmeal arrives, "I called the voice mail in the personals ad."

"Oh, my," says Phil as he takes off his glasses and begins to blow little spurts of air at the specks on his bifocals.

"And?" asks my sister.

"And," I say, "his name is Bernie. Actually Boy-knee. I'm not sure he is someone I should meet."

"Why?" Mia demands, her red hair bouncing as she turns toward me.

"Well, he has a terrible accent."

Phil hooks the wires of his glasses behind his ears and says, "Was he really a writer?"

"Yes. He writes theater reviews. I didn't leave a message. I just hung up." They both are staring at me as if I am a stranger who just appeared at their table. I begin to feel hopeless. Then I remember it is my turn to pay and put a ten on the table.

"Call him back." says my sister. "Perhaps if you listen to the message again..."

"Only if you have a notion to," says Phil, and he smiles a little half smile and blinks a long blink.

The oatmeal arrives. We talk between bites about our plans for the weekend. My sister says, "We are flying to DC to celebrate Samantha's birthday. When we asked her what she wanted for a gift she said, 'My Nana and Grampa.' So we just have to go."

"That's wonderful, Mia," I say.

"And you, Jo? What's your plan?" asks Phil.

"The Anita Brookner book I ordered arrived yesterday, and I could only finish the week's work by promising myself I would read it in its entirety on Saturday. And I might go out for a lobster dinner!" I could see the flat expression on my sister's face. "And I might see if Hilton can go to a movie," I added.

"Perhaps he is already going with his girlfriend," Mia says tersely. Then she smiles across the table. "What's your plan, Phil?"

"Well, I've invited some neighbors in for cocktails, and then we are all going to Lyric Theater. There is a woman I met at the golf course and she is coming, too."

"Why, Phil, you old cutup," says Mia.

That evening I call the voice introduction number again. Then I press the four-digit number to leave a message. I say, "Hi, Bernie. I'm not Venus de Milo but I would enjoy meeting you for a cup of coffee." I leave my name and number.

Weeks go by, no call from him, and my sister brings in another personals page. As soon as we file into the booth, Mia begins to read. "Man From Away but here to stay. Brunswick area. DWM, 59, ex-teacher, ex-accountant, now a writer, tax preparer, very artistic and outdoorsy. Seeking a sweet, honest, educated woman with a reasonably tidy life."

Phil says, "Now as Mother would say, 'Here's a match made in heaven.' Will you be calling this one?"

"Oh, maybe," I say with a sigh.. I hadn't the heart to tell them about my unreturned call to Boy-knee.

"Here's the usual," says the waitress as she sets down three bowls of oatmeal and a plate of grilled biscuits.

"Could I have a different jelly? I really hate grape jelly," I say, eager to change the topic.

"It is a rotten thing to do to a grape," says Mia. Then she and Phil talk about wines. I eat my biscuit and stare at the ad.

That evening I am gripped, as if by a fever, by the need to call this Man-From-Away and arrange to meet him. I'm sweet, honest, educated, and my life is reasonably tidy. And, I am lonely.

I dial the voice introduction personals number, and I punch in his four-digit code. I listen as an almost flat voice says, "Hi. This is Bob. I'm six feet tall, rather lanky, and I have a ready smile and brown eyes. I met my first wife on a cruise around the world, and we married in Zurich, returning to live in Philadelphia. I taught school, had two lovely daughters, and fifteen years went by. I decided to change careers, got an MBA in accounting, and worked for a firm in New York City. I'm semi-retired now, prepare tax returns the first part of the year. The rest of the time I'm writing the biography of my grandfather, a painter quite well known in his time. I love sunrises, the outdoors, swimming, dancing, the arts and literature. I like to get away in my brand-new canoe, and I drive down to Connecticut from time to time to see my granddaughter. If you would like to get together, please leave a message."

A recording of a youthful woman's voice comes on the line. "To leave a message for this ad, press one. To listen to similar ads, press two. To record an ad of your own, press three." I press one.

I speak in my sweetest, most honest and educated voice. "Hi, Bob. My name is Jo. We are nearly the same age and have similar interests. I'm a commercial writer, also working on fiction. I love sunrises, the arts, symphony and literature. I, too, have grandchildren. And I have been thinking that it might...er...would be nice to meet a gentleman to share friendship and interests." I am trying hard to concentrate. I realize that I should have written my thoughts down before calling. I forge on. "I'll be coming to Brunswick next Sunday to Maine Writers & Publishers Alliance, and if that's convenient for you, perhaps we could meet for a cup of tea or coffee." I leave my phone number and hang up. I hurry off and clean my entire house. I haven't been this nervous since sitting and waiting for an invitation to my senior prom. But now I do not sit and wait. Now, I know about the immense benefits of cleaning while in the throes of anxiety.

The next day the phone rings constantly with business. Along about three o'clock the caller says, "Hi, Jo. This is Bob. You called in response to my personal ad in the Telegram?"

"Oh, hi, Bob. Yes, I did. Er... how are you today?" I begin to rummage around my desk for his ad. Oh, God, what did he say about himself? What did I say about myself!

"You said you were coming to Brunswick on Sunday. What time?" he asks, matter of factly, as if we have talked a thousand times.

"I could meet you between two and two fifteen. My writers' group meets at three."

"Right there on Pleasant Street, isn't it?"

"Why, yes."

"I'll meet you in front of the building."

"Oh, no! Let's meet some place for tea." I am not about to get in a stranger's car. And I do not want to be seen by my fellow writers looking like a lady of the evening in the middle of the afternoon.

"Not much open on Sunday. How about Dunkin Donuts?"

I imagine us sitting elbow to elbow at a long counter. "No...er... how about McDonalds?"

"Sure, Jo." Then he asks me what color hair I have, what color eyes, and what model and year my car is and hangs up. I forget to ask what he looks like. I imagine a tall, thin, outdoorsy guy. His eyes will be hazel. There will be just a shadow of a dark beard beneath his smooth face. His teeth will be square, and his smile will be instantaneous.

On Sunday I arrive at McDonalds a little before two o'clock and park right in front, in full view of the entrance. It occurs to me that I have no idea what kind of car Bob will be driving. Suddenly, a tall man in a red flannel shirt knocks on my driver's-side window. "Jo?" he asks.

I am startled but manage to get out of my sports car gracefully, the way I imagine an educated woman would.

We walk inside and order drinks at the counter. The restaurant is not crowded, thank heavens! We go to one of the blue booths along the back wall.

I stare at this man sitting across from me. He is indeed lanky but does not look like an outdoorsy sort of guy. In fact, if I had not seen him in the parking lot, I would have sworn that he hadn't been outside for years. His skin has a grayish cast to it, and the area below his brown eyes is darkened and crepe-like. His eyes are lusterless and have a tendency to roll to the side like doll eyes. His red shirt is outdoorsy with tan leather ovals stitched on the elbows, like a professor turned woodsman.

Something comes over me, just cloaks me in a kind of ether. I realize that here we sit, two people just a year apart in age facing the specter of loneliness, of dying alone, and somehow this allows us to step out of our ordinary lives and reach out to one another. I feel a tenderness rise up and flush my cheeks.

"Tell me about your granddaughter," I say.

Bob smiles a crooked smile and fishes three photos out of his wallet, spreading them on the tabletop.

"Why, she is lovely, Bob. Isn't it a miracle to have grandchildren?"

Bob says, "She's three in that picture," gesturing to the one I am holding. He makes a noise in his throat like he has swallowed a whole plum. It is a gigantic gulp followed by air being forced out of his nasal cavity.

"Are you all right?" I ask.

"What's that?" asks Bob, as if nothing has happened.

So I go on. "I just took my grandson home to Lewiston. He is with me the first weekend every month. I love him so very much. You must wish your granddaughter lived closer."

"Well, when you get to be my age you make fewer wishes," says Bob, the faint light now gone from his eyes.

"But I am your age and I make lots of wishes!" I say.

Then he makes a sound like he is stifling an enormous sneeze. It rings out halfway up his throat and rushes out his nostrils.

"Are you all right, Bob?"

Again he looks quizzically at me and says, "What's that?"

"Do you have a sinus problem? I mean now that the buds are finally springing open."

Bob looks at me as if I am speaking Farsi. He presses a long, thin hand against the strands of hair on top of his head. "You are not very tall," he says and makes a strange snuffling noise at the back of his throat.

"That's true," I say.

Bob reaches into his shirt pocket, behind his glasses case and two pens. Whatever he wants is not there. "What's a commercial writer?" he asks.

"Oh, it means I write commercials. I write newspaper ads and radio jingles and TV ads, business collateral — advertising," I say. "I've had my own business since 1980."

Bob says, "I'm writing about my grandfather. Now that was my mother's father. That's how the artistic side got to me." He drones on for about ten minutes as listlessly as if I am not there.

Finally, I interrupt when he stops to clear his throat. "Gee, Bob," I say, "It's time for me to go." It's a quarter of three.

He walks behind me all the way to my car. Then he says, "Well, if you are ever in Brunswick, give me a call."

It flashes through my mind to ask him his full name, but I am far too sweet to ask that of a Man-From-Away. I wish I had called Hilton, whose rental is only a couple miles away, to see if I could stop by after writers' group.

Instead, I call when I get home. "Hilton, did you get the photos of the house I mailed to you?"

"Yes, deah. They arrived yesterday."

"It has a real charm about it, like a grand old lady poised in a curtsey. When can you come see it?" I add some hot tea to my china cup.

"Actually, an offer I made on a house here in Brunswick was accepted..."

I interrupt. "Oh, I didn't know you were that close to buying." I am so surprised I have to sit down, right on my kitchen floor.

"Never mind. You'll find something better suited for yourself. Say, I may be over next week. Shall we have supper?"

"Sure, Hilton," I say, trying to sound composed.

"Good. I'll bring Ondaatje's new book. It's stunning," he says. Then he says good-bye. I continue to sit on the kitchen floor, sipping my tea, trying to understand how I misunderstood about the house. I notice that the grate in front of the refrigerator is dusty, pull it off and scrub it.

Friday is a bit warmer, and Mia and I decide to walk outside the gym around the Boulevard next to Back Cove. There is a new woman in the program, and she follows us outside. "Mind if I tag along?" she says. I do mind, but I cannot find my voice. These walks are the only times I have to talk to my sister.

We walk down a side street by big frame houses and approach the cove where the cinder path has already begun. The ducks are plopped down at intervals and are eating breakfast. The city skyline is outlined by the low sun's neon. The fog bank is lying crouched at the mouth of the harbor. The breeze is from the northeast, and it brings me the sweet smell of molasses from the baked bean factory at the edge of the cove. We are breathing hard from dashing down the curved street. As the three of us establish a common stride, the young woman says, "Get a look at the ass in the spandex." She gestures at a jogger with her head.

Mia says, "Tight buns."

"Mia, really!" I say. She is always influenced by whomever she is with and, while I find this fascinating, it is sometimes shocking.

Mia laughs, saying to the young woman, "My sister is looking for a sweetheart."

"She won't find one here. The men at five o'clock are much younger, and there are miles of spandex. That guy we just passed is the exception this time of day. I've picked up two guys out here after work just this week," she says. I find myself looking at her out of the corner of my eyes. She is wearing shiny, black leggings with orange lightning bolts, a jogging bra and a loose-fitting jacket. She has a bushel of dark brown hair, all wavy and as active as a quarter horse's mane. She has flashing eyes, suggesting spontaneity, which her voice belies. She is telling Mia about the guy she found yesterday in her measured cadence, the way people speak English if it's not their first language.

I interrupt. "Aren't you afraid? I mean..."

"Of what? My husband?" she asks in her flat tone.

Mia takes one look at my face and says, "My sister worries about AIDS. Before that it was VD. My sister is celibate." I notice that Mia is walking like a pony, flicking her head back when she talks.

The young woman laughs. "If you think you're going to find a guy out here, you'll always be celibate."

Mia stops at the half-mile marker, stretching one foot forward, then the other. The young woman says, "Here, try this. Bend over, grab your ankles, and then straighten your legs. Feel the pull? And it's a perfect way to shove your ass up in the air with impunity."

Mia laughs, and I can't help but join in as the three of us upend ourselves like bottom-feeding ducks. We hurry back to the gym, and the young woman goes inside for the cool-down exercises.

"Let's stay out here and stretch," I say. "I want to talk to you about the Queen Anne house you showed me. My idea was that Hilton and I could buy it together."

"Really?" She tilts her head.

"Well...yes, but Hilton bought another house in Brunswick last week." I reach down and pull up on my ankles. "I just wanted to tell you privately before we get to breakfast with Phil."

"Well, it's your fault we no longer have breakfast alone," she says, and the breeze tosses her red hair forward around her face. Mia looks at her watch. "Got to fly. I'm due in at eight for a brokers' tour." She almost prances to her car.

The next Friday at the Miss Portland Diner, I make an announcement. "I've decided to place my own ad." I toss the sheet of paper right onto the table.

"Oh, is that so," says Phil, sliding into the booth.

Mia pulls off her jacket and snatches up the ad. She begins to read aloud as if we three are the only people in the diner.

Seeking SWM

SWF, petite, intelligent, writer, would like to meet intelligent, honest man, 50-60, who enjoys literature, walking, cooking, theater, symphony, good conversation and grandchildren. Must possess a sense of humor and do own laundry.

Mia sets the paper down, saying, "This is good."

Phil leans forward and removes lint from my T-shirt. "Are we to understand that last Sunday's meeting with Man-from-Away was...less than successful?"

"Yes, Phil. It was actually kind of sad," I say.

"But," says Mia, "you're not giving up this time. That's good." She calls over to the waitress. "We'll have the usual." Then she turns to me and says, "Toss out the bit about the laundry."

"I think it's important. Remember that dentist I went out with twice? Both times he came over with his laundry."

"That was twenty years ago. Men have improved since then. It sounds like a put-down," Mia replies.

Just then the waitress brings the coffee, teas and ice water. Her hairnet is askew, and one of her red dangling earrings is caught up in it. She looks right at me and says, "Dontcha change a word. It's purr-fick." Her lips are the same fire-engine red as her earrings. "How 'boutcha say oatmeal lover."

I say, "Gosh. Thanks. I hadn't thought of that."

"Be right back with the oats," she says, her smile revealing the gap between her front teeth.

Phil dips the corner of a napkin in his glass of water and begins wiping his lenses. "Perhaps you should add financially sound."

"Thanks, Phil." I'm getting more advice than I need.

Phil holds up his glasses and surveys them for lint. "Now, this ad is free, isn't it?"

"It is, Phil."

"Well then, I say yes to run the ad," says Phil and votes with his right hand held up above his head.

The ever-vigilant waitress appears and looks at Phil. "Want somethin'?"

Phil pulls his hand down and turns somber. "Just breakfast and don't forget the brown sugar," he says. "By the way, Mia, isn't it your turn to pay?"

She nods, too busy with the ad to look up. "We need to add something else to this ad. Raise your hand again, Phil, and get us a pen."

The waitress complies and continues to stand there, shifting from one foot to the other. Mia writes, saying aloud, "Non-drinkers, non-smokers only."

The waitress folds her arms across her bosom and says, "Cripes, now nobody's gonna call her."

I look down at the little tag on my tea bag. It reads, "Fools rush in where fools have rushed before."

The waitress sprints over to the cook's cubbyhole. We watch as she lines up the plate of biscuits and the bowls on her arm and hurries to our booth. "Here ya go," she says. "I'll be right back with the check."

"Give it to the redhead," says Phil, opening the strawberry jelly.

As soon as I get home I search for the personals page. Then I remember I taped it to the side of my new file cabinet. I pull it down to look for instructions on how to place an ad. There they are on the left-hand side: "To Place Your Free Ad." I delete the part about laundry, then call the 800 number and dictate the newspaper ad. A perky young voice tells me how to record and retrieve messages. It is not easy. After three tries at recording my voice message, I hang up, write a script about myself and call back, trying not to sound weird or desperate. In fact, when I play it back, I sound like the Queen Mother or perhaps a New Zealander like Hilton. The perky voice informs me, "The ad will run Sunday."

Two days later I am at the little market near my home at 8 AM to pick up the Maine Sunday Telegram. I dash back, past windows with drapes still drawn and gardens just coming alive with spring, down the hill and home. I toss out all the advertising flyers, looking for the personals. It is tucked inside another section. The headline is printed in blue block letters, "Voice Introduction Personals." I open it up and halfway down the page is my ad. I tape it to the file cabinet. In the row next to mine I see, "Black Fish of Love. Open-minded, funny, affectionate, SBM, 32, DQ mate, great smile. Seeking heavy-set woman, thirty to fifty, 200-250 lb. for dining, quiet times. Honesty essential." Now, what the heck is DQ mate? Dairy Queen? He wants a large lady to go to the Dairy Queen with him? And my sister said not to mention laundry!

I take the rest of the paper and sit in my big, new sofa chair with the gargantuan ottoman. That's when the phone starts to ring. I have already decided not to answer it, but to let the machine record the calls so I can compose myself before calling back. The phone clicks and I hear, "Halloo. My name is Leonard. I'm an attorney BUT let me explain. I work for the Volunteer Lawyers Project in Portland. I'm thirty-five years old. You didn't give your age, but you sounded so interesting. I spent a year after law school in England, and I am wondering what part you are from. I'd like to meet you for coffee.

Call me anytime today at 656-2323." Wow, I think, this is amazing! A financially sound lawyer calls first!

Beep. "Hi, my name is Conrad. I was born in St. Paul, graduated from Yale, moved to Portland last year. I noticed you enjoy cooking. My idea of a good time is being in my kitchen in big slipper socks making soup...or folding clean clothes." My goodness. I should have left in the part about no laundry.

I decide to walk back to the store because the New York Times will be in by now and then go out for breakfast. On an impulse I call Hilton to see if we can meet for brunch. He is out so I leave a message on his machine. I pick up the Times, walk the mile and a half to Miss Portland Diner, and eat alone.

Three hours later when I return, the phone message light is blinking its tiny, red eye at me. I press the blue message bar. The machine's voice says in its robotic way, "Hello. You have seventeen messages." Geeze! Then it begins to play them. Leonard the lawyer plays again, followed by the soup maker in slipper socks. Then there is a message from a man from South Berwick who belongs to the Book-of-the Month Club and wonders if I do, too. And a very elderly gentleman who sounds so terribly sad, and a man from The Ad Club whom I know — and he's married!

Beep. "My name is Alonzo. They call me the I-talian Stallion. (HEE HEE HEE). Don't let that scare you. I am really just a guy trying to have fun. Have I ever seen you at The Roundhouse at Happy Hour? Ya voice sounds familiar. Or maybe it was the Crisis Hot Line? Was you working there last weekend when I called? Anyways, I like ya voice. So call me up...525-6101."

Beep. "Jo, deah. Hilton. Sorry to have missed your call. I was out picking up the Times. Now I'm off to Center Lovell. Let's talk later." I could see him bending over his desk, then abruptly standing erect, picking up his keys and funny hat, and dashing for the door. I'm sad to have missed his call and sorry that he is visiting Center Lovell again. That's where his girlfriend Julia lives.

I pause the messages. I put the cow teakettle on to boil, measure out the Afternoon Darjeeling tea Hilton gave me and leaf through the book review section until the cow whistles at the boil. While the tea is steeping in my grandmother's Japanese teapot, I cross the room to play more messages. There is a call from Marian, who wants to know why I haven't called her.

Beep. "Hi. My name is Boy-knee. I'm a writa, too. I see youse like tear-ter. Me, too. I write tear-ter reviews. I'm a big reada, too. John Grisham's my favorite, but Lord Tennyson's poetry ain't bad neither. Ta git back ta me call 353-1111." Forget it, Boy-knee, you lost your chance with Venus.

Now it's Tuesday and I am listening to a call from a tuba enthusiast from Sebago Lake who is in a Twelve-Step Program, is taking it one-step-at-a-time, and is glad I don't drink.

Beep. "Hi, Jo. I have to start by saying your ad was very compelling. Then when I heard your voice, I knew you were someone I should meet. I am the intelligent, honest man you are looking for. My name is Marshall. I can't leave my number because I live with my elderly mother and she listens in on all my calls. I'll call back later. Bye."

Beep. "My name is Alan. You might have noticed my ad, not far from yours I won the Personal-of-the-Week Award and a gift certificate for flowers, which I will bring to you when we meet. Call me. 334-2324 and we'll decide on your place or mine."

As I listen to all these messages, I am struck by all the lonely people in the world — well, greater Portland anyway — who will call up people they've never met, looking for connection. I guess I am one of them.

I leave for a walk. Everybody walks by, two by two — today even the ducks are in pairs. I feel like I must be the only single on the planet. There is a brisk, northerly wind whipping up the water in the cove. A few stalwart souls dressed in wet suits are parasailing, or attempting it. The unpredictable wind catches them off guard, and sails and sailors lay flattened in the wake.

When I get home the phone rings. I let the machine answer it. Beep. "Hello. My name is Bob. I'm rather lanky, and I have a ready smile and brown eyes. I'm semi-retired now, preparing tax returns the first part of the year, and the rest of the time I'm writing a biography of my grandfather. I'm outdoorsy..."

Keep Praying
– *1997* –

I picked up the telephone and before I could speak her voice tumbled into my head.

"'allo? It's me, Sister Margaret. You want company, you?"

"Sure," I said, looking at the mountain of silver pieces I had set out to clean. "Where are you?"

"Down the gate 'ouse," she said as if I should know this.

"Do you remember where to park?" I asked.

"Of course!" she said. "I be right h'up."

I put on the kettle for tea and walked down the stairs to open the front door of my townhouse, one of forty built on Portland Pier.

Sister Margaret, my Dad's 80-year-old cousin, had been an Ursuline nun for more than fifty years. It was a cloistered order when she entered, but the modernization of the Church had changed all that. And though the Ursulines maintained their vow of poverty, Sister was allowed to have a car for transporting nuns to retreats and to doctors' appointments. Her father's money had paid for the car, which her brother grudgingly bought. The car was quite small for a woman of her height. She sped around Waterville daily to visit the sick, "my ladies" she called them, but the ladies were dying faster than she could befriend them.

Sister Margaret came around the corner holding on to her veil against the sea breeze. Her close-cropped, white hair fluttered at the edges. She has always looked to me as if a kid drew her: a round flat face, oversized glasses, stick legs and a square torso.

"GOD-gee-ous day," she called out. She was beside me briefly in the entry hall before bounding up the stairs. "I've been in retreat for t'ree days," she said. "I'm praying 'ard for guidance." She headed for her favorite spot — the balcony overlooking the marina.

"Would you like a cup of tea, Sister?" I asked.

"Me? I'd rather 'ave a tape player," she said. "You got one of those t'ings?"

"There's one inside the stereo cabinet."

"'aven't you got one to carry around?"

"Well, yes. The quality isn't great and..."

"Get it!" she said in her nun voice. "And I would like dat tea."

A few minutes later we were seated on the balcony, teapot on the table next to the cassette player. Sister rummaged around her tote bag, a lime green affair with black-plastic spiral trim. "One t'ing I do is pray to God on my tape and then 'e talks back to me. I learned 'ow to do dis...meditation."

"Really?" I said calmly, sipping my tea.

She pulled a cassette from the far reaches of her bag. "'ere is the tape. You can play it for us."

I was stunned. "This tape?" I asked.

"Of course, dis tape," she said, handing it to me.

I placed it in the machine and pressed the play button. Her voice clambered out of the speakers.

"'allo, God? Dis 'ere is Margaret. I am so discouraged, me. All the years I taught school ... now there is no more school. I need somet'ing more to do den visit my ladies. I 'ave no meaning in my life, me."

There was a great long pause on the tape. The fireboat went by clinking and clanking like a drawer full of silverware. I remembered the mountain of tarnished silver on my kitchen counter. The tape hissed; then I heard, "'allo, Margaret? Dis 'ere is God. You are on da right track. Keep praying, you."

I was rendered speechless. I didn't know what to think. For one thing I didn't know God was French Canadian!

Sister reached over and shut off the cassette. "Well," she said. "What you t'ink?"

Still flabbergasted I managed, "Gee, Sister, I'm so sorry that you are discouraged."

"Well, wouldn't you be? Did you 'ear what God said? "Keep praying!" I've been praying for fifty-two years, me."

Something wicked in me stirred. "May I play the tape a bit more?"

"Not now," she said. "Say, dis is good tea!"

I wanted to steal the tape. Play it for my sisters. And for friends. I thought; this tape must be mine.

We sat there in silence while I connived a way to get the tape. I decided to substitute it. I brought out my entire collection of cassettes. I opened the case, pulling out one after another, reading titles to Sister. I thought if I stirred them all around I could slip Sister's tape from sight.

I said, "I have some wonderful tapes you might like to borrow. This is a great lecture; you could enjoy it in your car." I swirled all the tapes like they were cards in the "Go Fish" game. I continued, "Here's an extraordinary tape — the music of Saint Hildegarde de Bingen. Are you familiar with her life and music?"

"No. You play tapes in da car, too? I 'ave one about the life of Saint Ant'ony. Oh, 'e is powerful before the t'rone of God," she said and reached into the maze of tapes to extract hers.

This was not easy. "Would you let me borrow the tape?" I asked.

"No! I want to play h'it on the way 'ome." She tossed it into the cavernous green bag.

I was becoming obsessed. "I could mail it back to you tomorrow, Sister."

"What's d'best way nort'? I get lost every time I leave 'ere."

"Come on. I'll lead you to the Interstate, Sister," I said. I couldn't give up the hope of getting the tape. We walked down the steps and into the parking garage. I said, "I'm fascinated by the tape —this dialogue with God. I'd really like to hear the whole thing, Sister." I was matching her stride on our way to her little maroon car.

"You know, I bet you like my journal. I write to God. And, God writes back."

"Lovely," I said. "But, I'd rather borrow the tape."

As we approached her compact car, Sister's hand and arm disappeared up to the elbow into her tote bag. She pulled out her keys and some folded sheets of composition paper. She opened one, glanced at it quickly and said, "You can copy dis one and mail it back to me."

My mind screamed, I want to copy the tape! Give me the tape! I said, "Thanks, Sister."

We glanced out at the harbor. The Portland Yacht Club was having a race and there were sailboats tacking across the waves like so many scudding clouds.

"You t'ink I could learn to sail?"

"There's no doubt about it," I said.

She had looked old today but a smile leapt up and pushed against her silver-framed glasses. "You kidder," said Sister, tugging at her veil and linking her other hand in mine.

Then I remembered the time Sister and Uncle Rollie climbed up into my sister Mia's boat. It was in a cradle in their backyard and higher than the house. The two white-haired cousins scurried up the ladder. I didn't dare follow. They called out that they could see "the steeple of the cathedral" and even had their lunch up there. Uncle Rollie died that winter before he and Sister got to go sailing. "I miss Uncle Rollie today," I said.

"I do, too, me," she said. "'e was a good guy. Never 'urt anybody. You were so good to 'im, you. And the way you loved 'im — now you can love me!" We stood there, holding hands, each in our own sea of loneliness.

I said, "Follow me and I'll take you to the Interstate ramp."

"Follow the leader," chimed Sister.

She got in her car and before I shut her door I said, "Drive carefully, Sister. I'll write in a few days." I hurried to my car.

It was late that night after shining all the silver when I remembered the folded piece of paper in my pocket. I took it out and read her fluid Palmer-method script:

Dear God,

You who see everything, see me before you.

You who hear everything, hear my prayer.

You who know all things, tell me what to do.

Then, several lines below, printed in capital letters, was this:

DEAR MARGARET, KEEP PRAYING, YOU.

GOD

The Renaissance Man
- 1998 -

I was just cleaning up after an early supper when the phone rang. I wiped my hands quickly on the dishtowel and crossed the kitchen to answer. "Hello?"

"Hi, Jo. It's Don Woodard."

"Hey, how are you?" We hadn't spoken for several years.

"I'm not great. Mae left me," he said, very quietly.

"Oh, I'm really sorry. Gosh, after all the rough patches over the years, I thought you were both...you know...fine again."

"She left me for a woman," he said, softly.

"Would you rather it had been with a man?"

"Yes," he whispered.

"Well, gosh, Donald, gone is gone. I mean...joining the circus is gone. Moving to Utah is gone. She's gone. I'm sorry to hear this. Are you OK?"

"No, that is why I called you. I'm falling apart."

My mind was racing. "You need a plan. OK, here's one. I'm having a birthday party at the end of the month. You can come! Ninety-five people are coming. I think you know some of them. Babs will be there." My mind was racing.

"Isn't your birthday in January?" he asked.

"Wow, you remembered! Yes, but I've had many a party when only a few people got through the snow. Once it was the band, the caterer, a few hardy friends, and me. Leftover hors d'oeuvres are useless. Now I have half-year parties. I'll be sixty and a half this month!" I remembered that Donald was ten years younger than me. "And, here is another idea. I'll cook you some chickens!"

"Let me cook chickens for you," he said. "How about this Friday night?"

We talked about where he lived now, less than a mile from my house. We talked about where I lived. He had actually been in my house once at a party, way before I owned it.

"Are the kitchen floor tiles still blue?" he asked.

"How can you remember?" I should not have been shocked. I should have remembered he had a brilliant mind — photographic. "You didn't lay this, did you?"

"No, I'd be embarrassed if I had. I'll bet it's chipped and maybe has a crack or two."

"How do you know that?"

"Because it is the wrong tile for a floor."

We talked awhile longer and set the time for Friday's chicken dinner. By the time we said goodbye, he seemed a bit cheered up.

Later that evening I remembered when I first met Donald Woodard. In 1978, I was directing an in-house ad agency for the Lee automobile dealerships. Mr. Shep Lee scheduled all meetings with staff at 7 AM, sometimes as late as 7:30. The commute from Yarmouth was a problem, even with a company car, because weather was often a problem. Shep suggested I move to Auburn and told me about a penthouse above Roger's Haircutters on Main Street being designed by the talented architect Steven Blair. I went to look at it. It was going to be amazing! It was a third-story barn with a loft, all exposed brick, a woodstove, sauna and an Arno-like view of the Androscoggin River that included a bridge and the splendor of the falls. I signed the lease. I asked Roger if there was any chance the company doing the renovations could be done any sooner, as my current lease ran out at the end of the month. His face said I don't think so, but his voice said, "You could ask. The crew is up there now."

I bounded up to the third floor and stepped into the living room with its enormous windows and thirty-foot beamed ceiling. I could see a couple of guys working, so I said, "Hi, I'm going to be the tenant. And I was wondering if there was any way you could have the apartment (I couldn't bring myself to say the word penthouse) ready by the end of the month?"

A fellow in a black watch cap with white wisps of hair and light-blue eyes stood up in the loft. "We'll be done in two weeks," he said, matter-of-factly.

I decided to summon up coquettish charm but didn't bat my eyelashes. "What if you guys hired more great guys and really went at it. Then when would you be done?"

"Fourteen days," said the guy in the black cap. And then he smiled and said, "I'm Don Woodard and that is my partner, Dave Peterson. See you in two weeks."

So much for charm! The penthouse was done in fourteen days.

I opened my own advertising agency in 1980 right there in the loft. Mr. Shep Lee with his many auto dealerships was my first client. I did not schedule appointments before 9 AM. Three years later, I bought a Victorian house in Lewiston and hired Donald and his partner to convert the bedrooms into studios and the third floor into an aerie for me.

I saw Donald from time to time at performances and, since we both loved to cook, in specialty grocery stores in Portland. Then for business reasons, I moved my company to Portland in 1985. That year

I responded to a Request For Proposal (RFP) from the community college, and there at the meeting was Donald! I didn't get the advertising project, but Donald and I did reconnect. After the meeting we sat, talking, on a bench on the campus overlooking Casco Bay. His two girls had grown up; his wife was a massage therapist. He was no longer a contractor, had given up his tile business when he lost sight in one eye, and was now teaching computer animation. He had reinvented himself yet again. I remembered that I'd asked him once, "How did you get to be a tile guy?"

"First you go to Florence and then to the Portland Library. It is all mathematics —and art," he'd said.

Friday came and it was drizzling a soft rain. I drove to his house about six. He came to the door in his customary garb: L.L.Bean canvas shirt, tan pants and two-toned leather loafers. I stepped in to the entry hall. The floor was a wonderful design with tiles of gray, coral and white. He had restored the nine-foot ceilings in the living room and dining room, refinished the wide floor boards, and painted the walls in soft colors from the early 1900s. The renovations didn't go much further than that, but it was an elegant start. The best to be said about the kitchen was that it had potential and a great gas stove. We had wine, he played his guitar, and then served me dinner at eight. I was ravenous. Luckily the chicken was scrumptious. It was only oven-baked thighs, but it had a delightful combination of herbs.

"What seasonings do you prefer?" I asked.

"I like cumin, chili, cayenne, curry…"

I interrupted, "And clove? And cardamom?"

Now he interrupted, "And there is chervil in the chicken rub!" Somehow this struck us as immensely funny. We both liked all the C spices!

"Donald, do you remember the first night I stayed in the penthouse, and you nailed the boarded-up entrance door shut at street level? You said if it still looked like a construction site, I'd be safe."

"And you were," he said, emphatically. In the candlelight, his eyes looked almost gray.

"I wasn't sure I could kick the door open in the morning, but I did the heel kick thing you showed me and it opened right up. Gosh, that was twenty years ago!"

"That was a great project," Donald said, passing the chicken platter to me. "And the crew loved your daily pitcher of martinis while we were finishing work on the second floor."

Between bites we told each other hilarious stories of jobs we had done that went wrong, talked about our favorite restaurants (his was George's in Bar Harbor) and about our vegetable gardens.

We were listening to tapes on a boom box on a dining room chair. "Do you recognize that musician?" Donald asked.

"Sure do! It's Lenny Breau. He played the guitar like it was a piano." We talked about his riveting performance twenty years ago at the Cellar Door, across from the "penthouse" and figured out we were both there that night. We talked about his Chet Atkins connection and Lenny's tragic death at the bottom of a pool on the top of an apartment building in LA.

After dinner we sat on the couch in the living room, and Donald began to weep. He wept about Mae, he wept about his estrangement from his parents and about his life. Sadness had moved into the room and sat between us. He turned to me with tears coursing from his pale eyes into his white beard, and said, "What I need to do is find an intelligent woman to share my life with, someone who reads and likes to travel. I need someone to talk with about music and art."

I was shocked. Here was a guy, falling apart in his own living room and looking for a girlfriend! "That's about the last thing you need, Donald. You need a shrink. You need to call your parents. You need someone to clean this house. You need a lawyer!"

He said softly, "I need you, Jo."

I could hear my own heart pounding.

Grampa Mike
– 2011 –

"Grampa Mike been sick," said my three-year-old great granddaughter, Nola. Our visits had started this way for months now. Her mother brings her to me every other Wednesday around eleven. We have lunch and play until her mother returns from work in late afternoon. Nola usually falls asleep on the way home and I go to bed around seven that night. We both get delightedly played out.

I had called her mother last night to see what she had told Nola of her grandfather's death on Monday.

"We're not sure what to say," said Marcie.

"I am sure she will talk to me about Mike as she has for the few last months," I said. "She told me about sitting with him on his bed. She senses something is wrong."

"I know. She loves him so much, but how can we explain death to her without upsetting her? What can we say that won't frighten her?"

"Well, the only idea that pops into my head is to tell her that we are born with a little star inside us. Then one day, we go back up into the sky. Would that work?"

"Great! We'll tell Nola just before dark tonight. Thanks, GG," she said hurriedly. "Time for me to help get dinner together. See you tomorrow. Love you."

Marcie and her husband live nearby, are each successful business owners and amazing parents. They are athletic, have tons of friends, and raised her stepsister. They are the kind of parents we all needed, still do.

The following day my beautiful grand-girls arrive a little after eleven. Marcie looks like a model stepping out of a magazine and onto my porch. Nola is wearing striped leggings, a ruffled skirt and a polka-dot top — every color in the Crayola box. She picks out her clothes every morning, this miniature of her beautiful mother — fashion gene and all. We three generations are like a three-story building where each floor is brighter.

Nola and I shout over and over, "Have a nice day at the salon, Mommy. See you later, Mommy." We always yell this in unison. It's how we begin our fun visits.

After a lunch of macaroni and cheese, which is routine, Nola goes to get her three favorite stuffed animals. They are waiting for her in the "magic room" hidden behind a bookcase. I had named the big orange cat Ginger Baker, the small-striped cat Buddy Guy, and the pink pig Wilbur (of course). They are all wearing training pants because Nola decided last month, "no more di'pers." Sometimes we play that they are naughty children. "Time out," she yells and lines them up on the couch. I call back, "Until Christmas." She nearly collapses laughing.

Today the stuffed friends are in a dance recital on the coffee table. Ray Charles' voice and piano fills the room. Nola looks at me, this cherished little Marcie, and holds Ginger above her head. Then she steps closer to me.

"Grampa Mike been sick."

"Yes, darling, I know."

"Now, he's a star."

"How wonderful," I say, and she throws her arms around me.

Then she steps back, close to the "stage" coffee table. She holds Ginger by his fluffy white paws and dances him back and forth. "Daddy carried me outside and we saw him."

"Oh, Nola, was he twinkling his love to you?"

"Yes, GG. He was the biggest star." The dance recital continues and then she asks, "Where's your mother?"

I reply softly, "She's a star, too."

"Can she see Grampa Mike?"

"Yes, I think she can."

"Can she touch his hand?"

"Yes, Nola, I think she can." She throws herself into my arms and I feel again the miracle of this child, her star shining brightly.

Made in the USA
Charleston, SC
27 June 2013